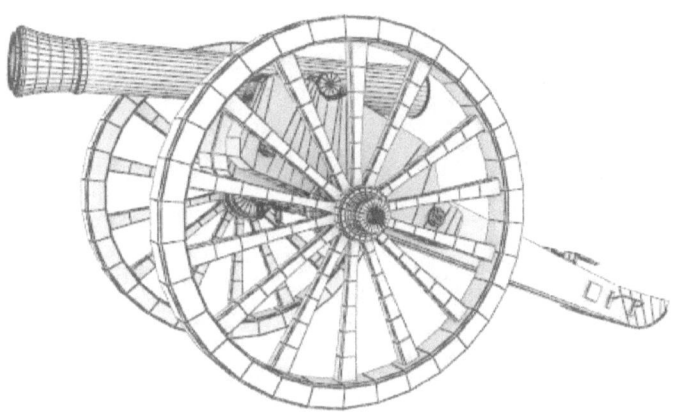

Cannon Law Firm

Guidebook To Oklahoma Criminal Law

By

John P. Cannon

Copyright © 2019 by Cannon Law Firm, PLLC

All rights reserved. No part of this publication may be reproduced, distributed, or transmitted in any form or by any means, including photocopying, recording, or other electronic or mechanical methods, without the prior written permission of the publisher, except in the case of brief quotations embodied in critical reviews and other non-commercial uses permitted by copyright law.

Please write to the publisher for permission requests, addressed: "Attention: Permissions Coordinator," at the address below.

PUBLISHING HOUSE

NightWriters Publishing

Ordering Info:

Cannon Law Firm, PLLC

Attn: John P. Cannon

600 West Sheridan Avenue

Oklahoma City, Oklahoma 73102

Printed in United States of America

1^{St} Edition 2019

FOREWORD

I wrote this book to help clients and their families facing criminal charges at every level of the justice system, particularly in Oklahoma. The book addresses the most common questions and concerns my Firm and other criminal defense Firms are asked, or should be asked, by every client and family of a client that walks in our doors. This book should not be taken as legal advice for your specific case or circumstance. Rather, it is a guide to facing the task of defending your case and seeking experienced, aggressive, and dedicated criminal defense counsel.

DEDICATION

I would like to dedicate this book to my clients and the attorneys of the Indigent Criminal Defense system, public defenders, who represent those that cannot afford to hire experienced criminal defense counsel. Specifically, I would like to thank the Oklahoma County Public Defender's Office that gave me, and some of the best defense attorneys in the state, the opportunity to fight for our clients in complex and interesting cases. All while maintaining professionalism and quality representation of many clients at one time. The years I spent as a public defender has forged in me a desire to constantly serve my clients with compassion and Fierce Advocacy!

All the adversity I've had in my life, all my troubles and obstacles, have strengthened me... You may not realize it when it happens, but a kick in the teeth may be the best thing in the world for you.

– Walt Disney

ACKNOWLEDGEMENTS

I would like to acknowledge the support, love, and patience of my family: my wife, Megan, and our three children. Their support allows me to spend weeks or long nights away preparing for and fighting for clients in jury trials. I cannot quantify my appreciation for the support they provide me every day, which makes it possible for me to pour myself into the lives and troubles of my clients.

Additionally, I would like to acknowledge the many paralegals in my legal career thus far, and in the future. My service to clients and this cause is greatly strengthened by your dedication and compassion.

Finally, I would like to acknowledge every criminal defense attorney, who helps defend our Constitutional rights, one day, one client at a time. The men and women in the Criminal Defense Bar are some of the finest and most selfless people you will ever meet.

There is no such thing as a self-made man. You will reach your goals only with the help of others. - George Shinn

9

TESTIMONIALS

"I signed up with John June 25th, July 5th. I received an email that my case is in line to be DISMISSED, within a 2 week time period. John made what was one of the most stressful times in my life better! Every case is different, but he handled my case with care and he was extremely open in his communication throughout the whole process. I hope to never have to have a criminal attorney again but if I do I will definitely go back to John. I highly recommend him to anyone else who is needing an attorney!"

Ashley

****

"John Cannon is an EXCELLENT attorney. He handled my case professionally and quickly. He is the first attorney I have ever met to take my situation and handle it without dragging it out occurring more expenses. I highly recommend him and will use him again if needed!"

A Former Client

****

"Hands down the best lawyer. Mr. Cannon accepted my case and got on it the same day. I would give him 10 stars if I could. I really appreciate the dedication on how he handles things with a short time frame."

Chris

****

"John Cannon assisted me through a very difficult time in my military career. He worked tirelessly with me on my case and kept me informed during the entire process. I can't say enough good things about Mr. Cannon. He's incredibly knowledgeable with regards to military justice. The outcome of my case was successful and I attribute that to Mr. Cannon's professionalism and expertise in dealing with military law. I would highly recommend Mr. Cannon to anyone with military justice or criminal defense needs."

Susan

****

DISCLAIMER

This publication is for informational purposes only. Nothing in this book constitutes legal advice. No attorney-client relationship is intended or in fact created by being provided a copy of this book or reading the materials contained in this book. The author assumes no liability for any errors, omissions, or detrimental reliance on material contained in this book. Please consult an experienced criminal defense attorney or other appropriate expert for legal or other advice.

Cannon Law Firm, PLLC
600 West Sheridan Avenue
Oklahoma City, OK 73102
www.JPCannonLawFirm.com

TABLE OF CONTENTS

Foreword	5
Dedication	7
Acknowledgments	8
Testimonials	11
Disclaimer	13
Arrest: The First 48 Hours	19
Miranda Warnings	28
Myths of Arrest and Defense Attorneys	25
Release from Jail and Beyond	29
Bail and Bond in Oklahoma	33
Arraignment	35
Your First Court Date and Beyond	39
Finding your Fierce Advocate	43
State Court Proceedings Overview	47
Federal Investigations	53
Federal Court Proceedings Overview	57
Federal Criminal Trial and Beyond	65
Military Criminal Defense Overview	69
Military Administrative Proceedings	73

Drug Crimes in Oklahoma	80
Driving Under the Influence	87
Your Driver's License After DUI In Oklahoma	93
Criminal Charges for Youth in Oklahoma	101
Property Crimes in Oklahoma	107
Assault & Battery Crimes in Oklahoma	111
White Collar Crime In Oklahoma	115
Factors In Going To Trial On Your Case	119
State Court Criminal Probation	123
Federal Sentencing & Beyond	127
Consequences Of A Conviction	139
Diversion Programs in Oklahoma	143
Can I Help My Attorney With My Case?	151
Attributes of a Great Criminal Defense Law Firm	157
Cannon Law Firm: Set Apart	161
Conclusion	163
Index	165
Testimonials (*Cont.*)	171
About the Author	175

ARREST: THE FIRST 48 HOURS

Being arrested is a confusing, stressful, and terrible experience, especially during the first 48 hours. The initial process can and will cause you and your family to have many questions, and it is important you know your rights and understand the process. You have heard of Miranda Rights in television and movies, but did you know it is actual law? You have the right to remain silent. You have the right to speak to an attorney. You have the right to stop speaking with law enforcement at any time. You have the right to have your attorney present with you when you speak to law enforcement. When your freedom and future are on the line, you cannot afford to risk speaking to police without your attorney.

Many of our clients have never been arrested before and this is their first experience having no freedom. Many worry about their safety, their future, and the effects of this experience. The most the average person knows about being arrested is from television, but fortunately, for you or your loved one, television exaggerates the process and the experience for entertainment purposes. In most counties in Oklahoma, including Oklahoma County and Tulsa County, upon arrest an individual will be processed at the office of the law enforcement agency/police department making the arrest, and then will be transported to county jail.

Upon Book-In, the police department or other law enforcement agency will notify the detention center (county jail) of the recommended charges, which are often highly exaggerated, and bond/bail is set based on a schedule determined by the District Court. Once bail is set by schedule, you may post your complete bail, a cash bond. which you/your family will have returned to you at the conclusion of your case. Alternatively, you can hire a bail bond company, a bondsman, to post the amount, and you will be required to pay the company a percentage of your total bond. Most bond companies require 10% of your bond, which the company will keep at the conclusion of your case. One wrinkle in this process can come from having charges or holds in more than one county, which an attorney can address for you.

Those individuals that do not post bond, either by cash or a bondsman, will stay in jail until released by the Court, or will be in custody until an attorney can seek an agreement on conditional bond, which does not require money in order to be released, or to have your bond reduced.

What Happens After I Get To Jail?

The book-in process is long and boring, with hours of waiting to complete tasks prior to being placed into an actual cell in the jail. Whether you bond out or not, you will be required to appear at arraignment, your first court date, either to receive your charges or be notified that charges have not been filed yet. At arraignment, you should enter a plea of not guilty, and if you have hired an attorney he/she can argue for your bond to be reduced or for more favorable conditions of being out of custody.

After arrest it will likely take hours before having access to "your phone call" to contact family or a criminal defense attorney. There is no time like the present to contact an experienced criminal defense attorney to begin fighting your case and reduce the damage in your case. I recommend contacting an experienced Oklahoma criminal defense attorney at the first sign of criminal trouble. Hiring a criminal defense attorney as a suspect, during the investigation, or before arrest maximizes your opportunity to minimize your exposure. A hired criminal defense attorney can contact the law enforcement agency investigating you and possibly stop the process, or help you avoid arrest.

Alternatively, if arrest is inevitable, your criminal defense attorney may be able to facilitate the time, date, and place you go into custody. This small amount of control can provide a great amount of peace of mind for someone anticipating arrest. Your attorney can contact the prosecutor, and appear before the judge assigned to your case, if a warrant is pending, and seek to have your case placed on the docket (receive a court date) without going into custody at all.

Common Errors After Arrest

Time heals all wounds, except being charged with a criminal offense. Often, time is the enemy of your criminal defense, as it offers more and more opportunity to make mistakes. The advent and spread of social media has resulted in hundreds, if not thousands of admissions and damaging statements being introduced against criminal defendants in Oklahoma. Whether you hire an experienced criminal defense attorney or not, be smarter than advertising admissions to a crime.

Talking about your case is the most common error criminal defendants make after being arrested. Phone calls are recorded in jail and used against defendants by the prosecution every day. Conversations can be recorded in Oklahoma, if one party consents to the recording. What does that mean? A person on their own accord or with assistance of police can choose to record a conversation with you, and turn that information/recording over to the prosecution or police. You should speak to no one on earth except your attorney about your case, period.

Does Hiring An Attorney Make Me Look Guilty?

Hiring an attorney is simply the smart exercise of a Constitutional right, to anyone associated with your case. You have Rights, you should use them. Police/law enforcement will not attempt to coerce a confession out of you or a loved one, if you are represented by counsel. Police know they cannot use a confession, if they question someone in custody without their attorney, assuming that person has hired an attorney. It is an irreversible error, a big problem, if anyone uses the fact you have hired an experienced criminal defense attorney against you in court.

Once you have been arrested, your only line of defense is your attorney. This is one right you do not want to waste. The first 48 hours may be boring; however, they may be far worse for your future, if you do not hire an experienced Oklahoma criminal defense attorney.

MIRANDA WARNINGS

In Chapter One, we looked at the consequences of being arrested or interrogated without having first hired an experienced criminal defense attorney. These issues have teeth in your criminal case, based on the Supreme Court decision in Miranda [1], in which the Supreme Court decided statements in limited circumstances are not admissible against criminal defendants.

There is a common misconception that Miranda Rights have a larger application than they in fact do. Information gained by interrogation which violates the requirements of Miranda may be used against an individual in their investigation; however, the words a suspect or criminal defendant say cannot be introduced at trial against the individual.

Although the application of Miranda Rights is limited; the remedy is clear cut, suppression. That means the prosecutor cannot present these statements to the judge or jury, if suppressed. In order to prove cause for suppression, two requirements must be met: you must be in custody, i.e. a reasonable person does not feel free to leave, and you are "under interrogation." Interrogation is a legal term of art in this context and does not cover all manner of statements police hear. Anything you say can and will be used against you, if you offer the information freely.

---

[1] *Miranda v. Arizona*, 384 U.S. 436 (1966)

Understanding the legal nuisances of Miranda Rights and suppression of improperly obtained statements/evidence is complicated and takes years to master. The fact that does not take time to master is exercise your right to remain silent. You and your attorney should speak before you make a statement to police.

MYTHS OF ARREST AND DEFENSE ATTORNEYS

This chapter was written to address some of the most common myths those facing criminal charges and their families have about arrest and hiring a criminal defense attorney. Often clients tell me during our first meeting they have already spoken to police and given their side of the story, or waited to hire an attorney because they did not want to appear guilty. More often than not, these actions do more harm than good. The following are myths I see or hear about on a regular basis. Hopefully, you will not make the same mistake so many have before.

MYTH 1: HIRING AN EXPERIENCED CRIMINAL DEFENSE ATTORNEY MAKES YOU LOOK GUILTY

Many myths exist concerning being arrested for an alleged crime, and about hiring a criminal defense attorney. The most common myth about criminal defense attorneys is that hiring one makes you look guilty. This could not be farther from the truth. Police, prosecutors, and judges assume nothing more than you know your rights and you are exercising them when you hire an experienced criminal defense attorney. You have rights, you should use them.

MYTH 2: ALL CRIMINAL DEFENSE ATTORNEYS ARE EQUAL

Another popular myth, all criminal defense attorneys are the same. However, experience, knowledge, and reputation matter with criminal defense attorneys just as with every other profession. An experienced criminal defense attorney has faced seasoned prosecutors and knows the tactics they will implement in your case. It takes experience to know how to weight the strengths and weaknesses in the prosecutor's case in order to advise a client about his/her prospects at trial. Experience never matters more than when your freedom is on the line.

MYTH 3: ANY ATTORNEY CAN DEFEND A CRIMINAL CASE

Another common myth, is that any attorney can defend a criminal case. A personal injury lawyer is not capable of handling an antitrust case, just as a civil attorney is not the best choice for your criminal defense. Defending criminal clients in State and Federal court is an art form, which requires experience specific to criminal law.

MYTH 4: CRIMINAL DEFENSE ATTORNEYS ARE UNETHICAL

Many view criminal defense attorneys as shady or suspect characters; this is another misconception. Criminal defense attorneys have the difficult task of balancing client interests with obligations to the justice system. Every profession has good and bad actors, but the majority of criminal defense attorneys are good, hardworking, dedicated attorneys that deeply care about their clients and their families. See what our clients say about our firm.

MYTH 5: I SHOULD TELL MY STORY TO POLICE

"When I'm arrested, I should tell my story to the police."

Myth. Many people accused of a crime want to immediately clear their name; they are wrong. It is important to present your side of the case; however, it is best to exercise this right with the assistance of experienced criminal defense counsel.

Often, a client will speak to police and corroborate or confirm some or all aspects of a charge they are facing without even knowing what they have done. Law enforcement can present charges to the prosecution on any crime they have probable cause to believe you or your loved one have committed. You should help your attorney defend your case; not help the police prosecute your case.

MYTH 6: POLICE HAVE TO TELL SUSPECTS THE TRUTH

Many people believe police are required to tell the truth; this is a myth. Police are allowed to lie and misrepresent facts during the course of an investigation. In fact, it is one of the most effective investigative techniques used. I would not mention it here, if it rarely occurred. Police have a job to investigate crime, but you are not required to make their job easier. You have the right to remain silent, exercise it.

MYTH 7: PUBLIC DEFENDERS ARE NOT GOOD LAWYERS

Public Defenders are not good lawyers; myth. As a former public defender, I have first-hand knowledge of the fact that Public Defenders are often dedicated and highly skilled attorneys, who choose to dedicate all or part of their career to public service. Public Defenders work solely in criminal defense, and although they have very large dockets, they are often very dedicated to their clients.

RELEASE FROM JAIL AND BEYOND

Although getting out of jail is a welcomed change in circumstance, it is far from the end of the road in your journey. If you are fortunate enough to get released on bail, a number of important things happen during your release:1) your property is returned to you (unless kept as evidence), 2) your bondsman or the sheriff's department will give you a bail slip detailing your bond, booking charges, and your initial court date.

Your initial court date, or your 'arraignment date', is very important. It changes based on whether you are in custody or not. A date you were told prior to release could very well be different from the date on your bail slip, trust the bail slip and contact an attorney. Often, your charges, if any, will not be filed by the first arraignment date due to overloaded dockets and over-burdened prosecution offices. It is important to keep track of your arraignment or first court date, and appear, unless you have hired an attorney and he/she advises otherwise. Failing to appear for your arraignment may result in a warrant being issued and your bond being increased or even denied.

The charges listed on your bail slip are important. Although, police or law enforcement can only recommend charges to the prosecutor, often the listed charges are very close to what the prosecuting office actually files against you in District Court. Understanding your charges, or better yet, your criminal defense attorney understanding your charges and explaining them to you, will increase your defense attorney's ability to advise you on what you may be facing after charges are filed, and how serious your case is in the eyes of law enforcement.

After you have been released, take a few hours to make contact with loved ones; go home; take a shower; and relax – for a few hours. Then, begin your research for an experienced, quality, criminal defense attorney. Look at attorneys' websites, written work, and what former clients say about their attorneys. You should not take the process lightly; it is key to your future that you hire an experienced criminal defense attorney.

What Should I Not Do After Getting Out Of Jail?

Do not investigate your own case. I repeat, do not investigate your own case. Criminal defendants have found themselves facing serious charges of intimidating and threatening witnesses for taking it upon themselves to investigate their own case.

Do not pick up a new criminal case. Everything is not lost based on being arrested and potentially charged with a crime, but you will make it more difficult for yourself, and your attorney, if you get yourself into more trouble after you are released. The fewer criminal charges you are facing, the higher the likelihood an experienced criminal defense attorney can accomplish a favorable outcome in your case.

Do not hire an attorney inexperienced in criminal defense for the type of charges you are facing. It is not important to hire an attorney that markets their work in criminal defense; it is important to hire an attorney experienced and talented in criminal defense.

Do not stop with going home and relaxing. Do your homework. Research, interview, and hire an experienced criminal defense attorney. Your future and freedom depend on it.

BAIL AND BOND IN OKLAHOMA

Although every misdemeanor and felony crime in Oklahoma is an arrestable offense, they also carry bond, except very serious violent charges. An offense that carries bond means you can get out of jail while your case is pending, if you or a bondsman post the bond. You, your family, or a loved one can post your bond directly through the Court, i.e. go to the jail or courthouse and post the cash for your bond with a cashier's check or cash.

It is important you keep copies of the receipt if you post a cash bond, as the bond will be returned or exonerated at the conclusion of the case, if the person appears for his/her court appearances, whether convicted or not.

The majority of criminal cases are resolved in three to six months, with exceptions, which means the money you gave to the court or jail will be returned in that same time frame.

However, due to a variety of reasons, the majority of those facing criminal charges hire a bail bondman. Typically, a bail bondsman requires you to pay them ten-percent (10%) of the total bail prior to the bondsman going through the process described in the previous paragraph (posting your bail at the jail or courthouse).

The bail bondsman will guarantee you or your loved one's appearance at all future court appearances. If you or your loved one fail to appear at court, the bail bondsman will be liable for the total amount of bail, and they may seek to recover the total amount from you. The bail bondsman will keep the percentage of bail you pay them at the conclusion of the case, regardless of the result, as opposed to the total amount being returned to you by the court/jail, if you post the bond. Ask around, check with the Better Business Bureau, and look at online reviews to determine the reliability of the bonding company or ask your attorney for a list of reputable bail bondsmen.

Many people arrested are released on conditional bond, which means they do not have to pay cash to the court or a bail bondman conditioned upon abiding by or performing a number of conditions. Additionally, in some counties or circumstances, individuals are released for non-violent offenses on their own recognizance, an O.R. Bond, which does not require any money being posted towards the bond.

Alternatively, you may seek a loan from a financial institution with collateral to get the cash for bond, which would save you the bondsman fee; however, a loan will take more time than a bonding company and comes with other costs, such as interests.

Regardless of how you or your loved one gets out of jail during the case, it is an invaluable tool for you and your attorney, if you are out of custody. As discussed in a later chapter, you can do much good for your case and your attorney out of jail.

ARRAIGNMENT

Arraignment is the first time you will appear before the Court with competent jurisdiction, authority, to answer for the filed criminal charges brought against you.

At arraignment, you will stand before the judge, hopefully with your hired criminal defense attorney, be informed of the charges filed against you by the prosecuting office, and be asked to enter a plea to the charges.

We previously discussed proposed charges by the arresting officer or law enforcement agency. The opinion of the arresting agency, their reports, and other information factors into the charges filed by the prosecuting office and, although the prosecutor must rely on competent evidence in deciding what charges to file, he/she has wide discretion on what offenses to file or allege against you. This discretion is sometimes exercised improperly, which an experienced criminal defense attorney can zero in on and fight against for you.

As discussed in chapter four, the arraignment date you received in custody may be incorrect. You need to hire an attorney or check on a regular basis with the judge handling the arraignment to ensure you appear at the right time, place, and date. Failing to appear for arraignment can result in your bond/bail being revoked and potentially denied. You will not be able to get out of jail without the assistance of an experienced criminal defense attorney, if your bond is denied.

In Oklahoma state court proceedings, the document used to charge you is called the Information. The Information lists the title of the crime or crimes charged; a brief factual summary of each charge, including; the date, the statutory reference for the charge; and the signature of an Assistant District Attorney filing the charge. In some counties, the prosecutor who files the charge will try the case; however, in other larger counties the prosecutor that filed the case may not ever be involved again.

The default plea at arraignment is Not Guilty. It is a non-confrontational appearance, and even if you and your attorney will seek a plea agreement from the beginning of your case, you should enter a plea of Not Guilty at arraignment. The prosecutor assigned to your case will likely not attend your arraignment; in fact, the other side may not ever be in the courtroom.

During In-custody arraignment or arraignment from jail, will typically be held by video or an informal proceeding with the judge. The judge will provide you the same information indicated above; however, the time frame for arraignment for those in custody is much shorter than out of custody defendants. If charges are filed against you and you were never arrested a warrant will be issued for your arrest. Although this is sounds scary, you can avoid arrest by hiring a bail bondsman to conduct a "walk-through" with you at the county jail. The process takes a few hours, as the information needed by the jail is collected, but you get to walk out of the jail the same day with your bail bondsman.

Arraignment is the first official date you face the charges filed against you, and in additional to the information previously discussed, the judge will advise you of your Constitutional Rights at arraignment: rights you should discuss at greater length with your criminal defense attorney. If your case is a felony, you and your criminal defense attorney will be advised of the assigned District Judge.

Often, the prosecutor handling your case will not even get your file until after you are arraigned. Once your criminal defense attorney identifies the prosecutor handing your case, he or she will be able to begin working towards the best possible outcome for you.

YOUR FIRST COURT DATE AND BEYOND

Time is critical and you should act fast. Your first court date, your arraignment as discussed in chapter six, will be within a week if your bond is denied or you do not post bail. Unfortunately, the length of time until your first court date while in custody is based partially on when you were arrested. It is true you do not want to be arrested on the Friday night of a holiday weekend, because you may have to wait four or five days to see the judge. However, if you post bail, your first court date will likely be within 30 days after your release.

Whether you are in or out of custody, your first court date will be much smoother with an experienced criminal defense attorney. Your attorney will be able to appear on your behalf, meaning you will not have to go to court, or you will have your case heard at the beginning of the docket, which will allow you to leave the courthouse shortly after arriving.

At arraignment, the Judge will advise you of your charges and ask "How do you plea for purposes of arraignment?" Your answer, regardless of whether you plan to fight your case or work out the best deal possible should be "Not guilty, Your Honor." After you enter your plea the Court will notify you of the first court date before the judge handling your case. In the interim, your defense attorney should contact the prosecutor assigned to your case and begin fighting for you.

How Often Should I Meet with My Attorney Between Court Dates?

Although you may want to meet with or receive updates from your criminal defense attorney on a regular basis, the fact is your attorney generally must wait for information from the prosecutor, which takes longer than either of you would like to wait. In some cases, things move very quickly and you will receive information and have phone/email exchanges from your attorney on a very rapid basis. In other cases, you and your attorney must wait from fifteen (15) to forty-five (45) days for useful information from the prosecutor. The seriousness, complexity, and amount of charges you and your criminal defense attorney are facing plays a major role in the length of time you must wait for answers.

Although your attorney has the ability to request police reports directly from the law enforcement agency which is or has conducted the investigation into your case, the information provided directly to your attorney is limited. You will not learn everything you want to learn about the prosecution's case against you until your criminal defense attorney is able to meet with the prosecutor. During that meeting your attorney will discuss the circumstances warranting a better outcome for you, the discovery or reports by law enforcement, and how the prosecutor sees the case.

It is important when interviewing criminal defense attorneys to get an idea of how long they think it will take to have real answers about the process in your case. You are entitled to know at the very least the following: what attorney will be personally handling your case, who can you speak to in the firm, what is the timeline going forward, and what are reasonable expectations.

FINDING YOUR FIERCE ADVOCATE

If you or your loved one are currently facing or potentially facing criminal charges, now is the right moment to hire a criminal defense attorney. No matter where you are in the process, it is never too early to be represented by experienced criminal defense counsel. You cannot change the past, but an attorney can help you change your future. Without an attorney you may dig yourself into a deeper hole without even knowing it. As discussed in previous chapters, police and investigators will not tell you that you are providing them more for their investigation against you until it is too late, or never.

How you handle the investigation in your case may dictate your future. You need more than a criminal defense attorney, you need a Fierce Advocate, preferably one with a wide range of experience and a track record of success for clients, and with respect from prosecutors and the bench.

The right answer is always to hire an experienced criminal defense attorney as soon as possible, if you are being investigated for a crime or have already been arrested or charged. Even a suspicion of being investigated is cause to hire an experienced defense attorney. The fee for representation during a potential investigation will be far less than after criminal charges are filed, and being represented during an investigation may protect you from charges ever being filed against you.

This is a smart investment. The exercise of your right to hire a qualified and experienced criminal defense attorney can never be used against you in an investigation or court. Further, it offers benefits throughout the investigative phase of your case that you would not have without an experienced attorney. Although you cannot control whether or not you will be arrested or charged, you can dictate an aspect of the procedure by hiring an experienced criminal defense attorney.

A dedicated criminal defense attorney will reach out to interested law enforcement and advise them that you are represented by counsel and should not be contacted except through your attorney's office. My firm requests investigators, police, and law enforcement direct all questions and requests of our clients to my office and in writing. An experienced criminal defense attorney can act as a protective barrier from missteps with police, such as unintended confessions and police contact before you are prepared to tell your story.

Generally, without an experienced criminal defense attorney you will not be able to forecast law enforcement's actions or investigation. However, with our office you may get a preview of law enforcement's intention or the course of their investigation prior to or without appearing for an in-person, possibly highly damaging interrogation.

Again, Law enforcement is not legally obligated to tell you the truth. In very limited circumstances, your attorney can use law enforcement lying to you against the prosecution's case; however, it generally will not help you. The opposite is not true; any and every misstatement, mistake, or lie you make to police/law enforcement will be used against you! You cannot make a mistake when talking to police. The safest bet; do not speak to police, hire a criminal defense attorney that knows their business. Then and only then should you consider the option of telling your story to law enforcement. An experienced criminal defense attorney cannot change the facts; however, your defense attorney can advise you, if you should tell your story or simply force the prosecution to attempt to meet their burden, beyond a reasonable doubt, at trial.

What Can a Defense Attorney Do Before Charges Are Filed?

As discussed in the previous chapter, an experienced and dedicated criminal defense attorney will notify the law enforcement agency investigating your case that you are represented by counsel, should not be contacted directly, and that requests should be submitted through your attorney's office. Although prosecutors and police are not obligated to comply with your attorney's request, if your attorney has earned a reputation of respect he/she may be able to find out the contemplated charges and other useful information for your defense.

Your attorney, as your advocate, can begin to tell your story to law enforcement and/or the prosecutor, without you making a statement. This information could prove your innocence, which would stop charges from ever being filed, and save you and your family substantial time and stress. Your attorney can provide information to convince the prosecutor to file or law enforcement to present less serious charges. Your attorney can cast doubt on the credibility of witnesses, or provide contact information for witnesses beneficial to your case that should be interviewed before a decision to charge you with a crime has been made by the prosecutor.

Finally, the right criminal defense attorney can investigate your case before favorable statements are forgotten by witnesses, or erased from their memory due to substantial contact with investigators building a case against you. Although witnesses are not obligated to speak to criminal defense investigators, it is always a useful process to pursue. I have seen cases won or greatly improved for my clients by the information discovered or exposed by the dedicated investigators I have worked with over the years.

You need a Fierce Advocate. Your case and your future depend on hiring the right attorney for the job. Do your homework, interview attorneys, and prepare to fight your case.

STATE COURT PROCEEDINGS OVERVIEW

Although every Oklahoma state court criminal proceeding varies from the next, there are general aspects of the process that do not change.

Before going through this procedural overview, you may ask what factors cause the process to vary from case to case: here are some of the most common causes for the process to vary; specific procedures for the county in which your case is pending; the docket and judge assigned to your case; the prosecutor handing your case; and the volume of cases on the docket.

Now to the overview.

- Arrest: the jail or sheriff's department will set your initial bond based on the presumed charges presented by the arresting agency. The prosecution office will decide your charges; however, law enforcement must present charges for bond to be determined. The jail will use a predetermined "bond schedule" that includes every crime in the book to set your initial bond. Next you will go through in--processing, which may take over 12 hours, during this time you should be allowed to make a phone call and will be assigned a cell in the jail. It is crucial you contact someone who can assist you in retaining criminal defense counsel and a bondsman, if you have the funds for both.

- Process Initiated: the involved law enforcement officer or officers draft a citation, proposed charges, or simply police reports, which are given to the prosecutor's office to review and consider charges.

- Prior to Arraignment: It is crucial to obtain an experienced attorney in the time between arrest and charges being filed. An attorney can begin investigating your defense, preserve important evidence, begin communicating with the prosecution's office, and illustrate evidence or witnesses to law enforcement that should be investigated.

- Arraignment: The Court will provide you with a copy of the actual charges filed against you by the prosecutor, notify you of your initial court date before the assigned judge, and the Court may hear your attorney on reducing your bail. Additionally, if not already identified, your attorney will be able to determine the assigned prosecutor on your case and begin communicating with him or her about your case.

- Preliminary Hearing Conference: Your attorney and the prosecutor will discuss your charges, your case, and do one of the following: set the case for preliminary hearing, begin negotiations, reach a plea agreement, or dismiss the case based on information provided by your criminal defense attorney.

- Preliminary Hearing: You have the right to a preliminary hearing pursuant to Oklahoma Statute Title 22 Section 258. The prosecutor has the burden of proof at the preliminary hearing; however, the burden is much lower than at trial. The rules of evidence apply, but your attorney may strike harsh blows to the prosecution's case, if prepared. It is essential to have an experienced attorney defend this stage of your case.

- Pretrial Conference: You and your attorney will appear before the District Judge that will conduct the jury trial in your case, if you decide to take that route. Additionally, your criminal defense attorney will continue working on the prosecutor of your case. You now have the options of reaching a plea agreement, fighting your case, or entering a blind plea and arguing the sentence of your case to the District Judge.

- Jury Trial: A jury panel is selected after your attorney, the prosecutor, and the judge ask the venire, potential panel, questions. The prosecution has the burden to prove your guilt beyond a reasonable doubt and the jury must be unanimous. Your attorney is allowed to question every witness and piece of evidence presented by the prosecution. Your attorney will present your case to the jury and should fight for your innocence by attacking weaknesses in the prosecution's case and by telling your story.

- Verdict: The jury will return a verdict. Upon a not guilty verdict, you will be released from any further proceedings. Upon a guilty verdict, your case will be set over for sentencing and you will remain in custody or be placed in custody, unless the judge grants your attorney's request for release pending sentencing.

- Sentencing: Your attorney has the opportunity to present evidence and witnesses in mitigation and extenuation on your behalf whether at the conclusion of a trial or based on a plea.

- Appeal: upon a guilty verdict, you have the opportunity to appeal to the Court of Criminal Appeals. Your criminal defense attorney can raise any issue for consideration, including prosecutorial misconduct, rulings by the Court, and other errors that negatively impacted your case.

- Although this summary of proceedings is based on state court felony proceedings, the majority of this process is applicable to federal criminal practice, misdemeanors, or city charges… however, the months leading up to your trial are essential in order to develop and build your compelling story; in order to tell that story at trial.

FEDERAL INVESTIGATIONS

How Are Federal Investigations Conducted?

Multiple federal agencies have criminal investigative units, or divisions, that collect and provide investigations to the United States Attorney's Office in the Federal District in which the events occurred. Despite the common perspective, that the Federal Bureau of Investigation ("FBI"), the Drug Enforcement Administration ("DEA"), and Bureau of Alcohol, Tobacco, Firearms and Explosions ("ATF") conduct all federal criminal investigations, most federal agencies have a federal criminal investigative unit. However, the majority of federal criminal investigations are indeed conducted by the following federal agencies:

Federal Bureau of Investigation (FBI)

Drug Enforcement Administration (DEA)

Bureau of Alcohol, Tobacco, Firearms and Explosives (ATF)

United States Secret Service (USSS)

Homeland Security Investigations (DHS/HSI)

Federal Investigators v. State Investigators

Federal investigators work under a similar framework as local and state law enforcement; however, their authority is based on federal regulations or statutes. They have areas of interest, such as the Internal Revenue Service ("IRS"), whose investigators primarily investigate tax fraud and financial crime, i.e. white collar crime. Federal investigators interview witnesses, collect evidence, and assist federal prosecutors, United States Attorneys, in understanding the facts of a particular case, and oftentimes United States Attorney's Offices work with multiple, separate, federal agencies in one investigation.

Search warrants are often requested in the course of federal criminal investigations. You have Constitutional protections under the Fourth Amendment that require probable cause before law enforcement can search your home, your person, your car, or other property, and a "neutral and detached" judge must sign a search warrant prior to it being executed.

Federal arrests and searches are primarily conducted after an arrest warrant, based on probable cause, is signed or issued by a federal judge. Local and state investigators often conclude investigations with a search warrant being executed; however, the majority of state criminal cases come from arrests by local law enforcement and subsequent searches. Federal agents do have the authority to arrest an individual at the time a crime is committed, if probable cause exists, just like state and local law enforcement; however, more often than not Federal agents act upon investigations, not simply contact with alleged suspects.

The evidence collected in the course of federal investigations is similar in form to the evidence collected in state and local law enforcement investigations; 'direct' and 'circumstantial' evidence.

Direct Evidence: the statements, photographs, video, and other information obtained during a federal investigation is reviewed and evaluated against federal law and jurisdiction by United States Attorney's Offices to determine if sufficient evidence exists to present to a Federal Grand Jury. Direct evidence supports a fact without an inference, such as eyewitness testimony, including a person's claim they actually saw a crime occur. However, testimony of something before or after an alleged crime is circumstantial evidence.

Circumstantial Evidence: all indirect information relating to a criminal act – as stated above, information before or after a crime – is circumstantial evidence. It requires an inference, or a leap from a fact known to a fact assumed.

Some state court criminal investigations consist of coordination and back and forth between District Attorneys and law enforcement over a period of time; however, generally law enforcement conducts its investigation separate from state prosecution offices. Alternatively, in federal criminal investigations the United States Attorney's Office almost always works alongside federal criminal investigators during the course of the investigation, which facilitates Federal criminal charging decisions in United States Attorney's Offices. An experienced criminal defense attorney will make contact with the federal investigators in your case as well as the United States Attorney involved to advocate your position prior to a charging, indictment, or grand jury decision is reached.

FEDERAL COURT PROCEEDINGS OVERVIEW

Federal prosecution is based on events that cross state lines or violate federal regulations or United States Code. Generally, state criminal proceedings cover all manner of criminal conduct, and only a limited amount and type of criminal acts are to be prosecuted or handled by the federal government; however, the size and breadth of the federal government and its interaction with citizens everyday has led to a substantial number of acts, which are prosecuted or handled by federal prosecutors and federal law enforcement.

Federal Criminal Charges

After federal prosecutors review the completed investigation from federal criminal investigators, they may interview witnesses or involved individuals and then make a decision to present or not present the case to the Grand Jury.

Upon Indictment, the formal notice that federal prosecutor(s) believe a suspect has committed a federal crime, the suspect is notified of the federal criminal charges against him or her. A Grand Jury, a group of impartial citizens, is called and hears the evidence against the suspect. During the grand jury, witnesses are called to testify, evidence is presented, and the federal prosecutor presents a summary of the case to the grand jury members. No indictment comes from the Grand Jury if they believe insufficient evidence exists.

The United States Constitution specifically provides the right to a Grand Jury for certain criminal offenses. The purpose, if not obvious, is to provide a criminal defendant an unbiased decision about the sufficiency of the evidence against him or her prior to being forced to face the rigor of federal prosecution.

Grand Juries consist of 16-23 members, and the proceedings cannot be viewed by anyone not specifically authorized to attend. After the Grand Jury members hear the federal prosecutor's case they vote in secret, which determines whether or not the federal criminal defendant will be charged with a crime.

All Grand Jury proceedings are sealed, which means no one except the individuals in the room know who testified, what they said, and what evidence was presented. Witnesses called to testify cannot have counsel present. At least 12 members must agree in order for an indictment to be issued.

Many states use the federally enacted indictment and grand jury proceeding; however, Oklahoma for the most part does not use Grand Juries for State misdemeanor or felony prosecution. Subsequent to a criminal defendant being indicted and charged with a federal crime, he or she can hire a federal criminal defense attorney, if they have not already, or be represented by a Federal Public Defender, if they qualify as indigent. A federal criminal defense attorney is vital to understanding the federal criminal charges and the federal criminal process, including trial and sentencing.

First Steps After Federal Charges

One of the protections all federal criminal defendants exercise is the right to being tried in the location or venue a criminal allegation takes place. Federal criminal cases are tried in one of the 94 Federal District Courts in the United States. Oklahoma is one of the few states that has multiple federal districts, in fact we have three: The Western District of Oklahoma (Oklahoma City), The Northern District of Oklahoma (Tulsa), and The Eastern District of Oklahoma (Muskogee). Although a federal criminal charge may be related to criminal allegations anywhere in Oklahoma, the case will be tried in one of these three federal courthouses.

Initial Hearing

The federal criminal system is more efficient and moves faster than state criminal procedures. The day, or day after, a federal criminal defendant is arrested they will be brought before a magistrate judge for their Initial Hearing. The criminal defendant will be asked to enter a plea of guilty or not guilty to the charges against him or her. Otherwise, this proceeding is mainly informative to the criminal defendant. He or she will be notified of the charges brought, his or her rights, and the magistrate judge will determine his or her custody status during the pending federal criminal case, i.e. release or jail until trial.

An experienced federal criminal defense attorney can assist you in obtaining release during your pending criminal case in federal court. The magistrate judge will consider a number of factors in determining whether or not the criminal defendant meets the factors for release via bail, which includes holding a hearing to determine the following factors:

Defendant's threat to the community;

Defendant's ties to the community;

Defendant's length of time in the community;

Location of Defendant's family;

Prior criminal record;

Whether or not threats have been made to witnesses;

At the conclusion of the hearing, the magistrate judge will determine whether or not the individual can put up funds for release to ensure their return. If not, the defendant will be remanded to the custody of the U.S. Marshal's Office until jury trial. During this time, the individual will be held at a federal facility, hopefully in close proximity to the federal court in the respective district.

The Discovery Process

The majority of the time and effort in a federal criminal case is after arraignment, but before federal criminal trial. Both sides will contact witnesses to learn how they will help, or more importantly, hurt, that party's case, and both sides will be providing the evidence they intend to use at trial. This process is called Discovery and is an ongoing process of "discovering" material/evidence/witnesses, as well as providing information to the other side.

Federal criminal investigations are more substantial than a DUI or Larceny case, as hundreds of pages of discovery and material are generated, which your defense attorney must review in detail. Although the federal prosecutor who participated in the process will be familiar with much of the evidence/case against the federal criminal defendant, a federal criminal defense attorney will not have access to this information until after arraignment.

Federal appellate courts have developed substantial case law, based on common sense, fairness, and the Constitution, which requires the government to provide evidence to the criminal defendant that may help as well as hurt their case. Evidence that may help a criminal defendant's case is called exculpatory evidence. Failure of a prosecutor, whether intentional or accidental, to provide exculpatory evidence may result in sanction, fines, and potentially dismissal of charges or a new trial.

Can I Get A Deal On A Federal Criminal Case?

One of the benefits of exchanging discovery, as discussed in the Discovery Process, is the development of a great understanding of the strengths and weaknesses of the government's case. Meaning, as Discovery progresses, the Assistant United States Attorney(s) prosecuting the case and the federal criminal defense attorney representing the defendant will exchange information and ideas concerning the case. Whether the government has a strong or weak case, it may offer to either reduce the criminal defendant's exposure to the lengthy sentences included in federal sentencing statutes, or to avoid a trial the government may or may not win.

In order to enter a plea of guilty, the federal criminal defendant must actually have committed the crimes to which he or she is pleading. The defendant will be required to testify concerning their admitted crimes in a detailed proceeding, discussed in Federal Sentencing, unlike state and municipal criminal pleas in which the defendant may only be required to state the plea entered, i.e. Guilty or No Contest.

Upon entering a plea of guilty, a federal criminal defendant gives up many rights, including the government being required to prove their guilt beyond a reasonable doubt to a unanimous jury. Additionally, the federal criminal defendant consents to being sentenced by the federal judge presiding over their case. Prior to a plea being entered, the United States Attorney's Office may agree with the federal criminal defense attorney to not recommend an enhanced sentence; however, the federal judge presiding over the case has sole authority to determine the defendant's sentence.

The most important preparation by the defendant's criminal defense attorney in a federal criminal case occurs after entering a plea, if the defendant forfeits his or her right to trial.

Preliminary Hearing

Sometimes, but not always, the presiding judge will hold a preliminary hearing. Similar to the Grand Jury proceeding, the federal prosecutor will be required to show sufficient evidence exists to charge the defendant with the crimes, to which he or she is pleading. This right belongs to the defendant and it is waivable. Additionally, the preliminary hearing must be held within 14 days if the federal criminal defendant is in custody, or within 21 days of initial appearance if the federal criminal defendant is out of custody.

Federal court preliminary hearings are similar to state court preliminary hearings. The Assistant United States Attorney, prosecutor, will call witnesses and present evidence. Additionally, your federal criminal defense attorney can cross-examine and impeach the prosecutor's witnesses. However, unlike state court, the Assistant United States Attorney can introduce some evidence regardless of objection by your federal criminal defense attorney.

At the conclusion of the Assistant United States Attorney's presenting evidence, similar to state court preliminary hearings, the judge will decide if probable cause exists that the criminal defendant committed a crime. Trial will be held in the near future, if probable cause is found, or the judge will dismiss the case if he/she believes probable cause does not exist. Your federal criminal defense attorney can have a substantial effect on the outcome on this important part of the process.

Before Trial

Motion practice, in which your federal criminal defense attorney raises issues for your trial judge to decide upon and respond/object to motions or requests of the prosecutor, is a very important part of your federal criminal case. The judge will hear argument, if requested, or simply rule on every issue your federal criminal defense attorney raises. Pre-trial motions can take a variety of forms, and request an even wider variety of relief. The effect of pre-trial motions in federal criminal trial include: courtroom, the defendant, evidence, witnesses, testimony, and the trial itself. Some of the most commonly litigated pre-trial motions in federal criminal trial are often variants of the following:

Motion to Dismiss: federal criminal defense attorneys can seek to dismiss the case for a lack of evidence or illegal search & seizure issues by federal investigators.

Motion to Suppress: federal criminal defense attorneys can seek to suppress or keep out evidence, information, testimony, or witnesses, which is improper for a variety of reasons.

Motion for Change of Venue: federal criminal defense attorneys can seek to have a federal criminal trial heard in another federal district for a variety of reasons, such as pretrial publicity or prejudice in the district in high profile cases.

Although some motions cannot be resolved until issues occur during trial, an experienced federal criminal defense attorney can gain laser focus on the issues at trial by seeking and obtaining left and right limits on a variety of issues from the judge overseeing federal criminal trial. It is important to hire an experienced criminal defense attorney for your federal criminal defense that has knowledge of the federal criminal process and defenses available in your case.

FEDERAL CRIMINAL TRIAL AND BEYOND

Federal criminal trial proceedings and the evidence or information admitted at trial is controlled by the Federal District Judge overseeing your trial. The Federal District judge decides the evidence that is admitted or not presented to the jury and what the prosecutor and your federal criminal defense attorney can or cannot say to the jury. All the work done by your chosen federal criminal defense attorney will put you in the best position possible, or not, to be ready to try your federal criminal trial.

Your federal criminal defense attorney will have reviewed and be intimately familiar with all the evidence, witnesses, testimony, exhibits, and issues in your federal criminal case. The United States Attorney's Office prosecuting your case has the highest burden in any court in the United States. The prosecution must prove your guilt of each offense beyond a reasonable doubt in order for you to be convicted. The preparation of your federal criminal defense attorney and his/her ability to impeach the prosecution's case and tell your story may decide the outcome of your case.

The first opportunity for your attorney to begin presenting your case before the jury is during jury selection, Voir Dire. Your attorney will participate in selecting the jury from a "pool of potential jurors," often called the venire. Your federal criminal defense attorney will help the judge ensure that no prejudice is shown in selecting jurors, i.e. only women, only men, or the exclusion of a specific group of people. Both the prosecutor and your federal criminal defense attorney will ask the court to excuse jurors for cause, as well as without stating a reason, which are "Preemptory challenges."

The first portion of a federal criminal trial that is likely familiar to most people is opening statements. Jury trials are about stories, for a number of reasons, including that is how people are wired to learn and remember information. Your federal criminal defense attorney's ability to tell a convicting story before any evidence is heard and build on that during trial is key to reaching the best possible outcome in your federal criminal trial.

The United States Attorney's Office has the burden of proof, and as a result the prosecution presents its case first in order to attempt to meet its burden. Your federal criminal defense attorney can impeach and attack the credibility of information presented by each witness during the prosecution's case. Once the prosecution rests, your federal criminal defense attorney may move for the federal judge to determine as a matter of law that the prosecution has failed to meet its burden on some or all of the prosecution's federal criminal case.

The federal judge will dismiss any charge he/she believes the prosecution has failed to prove. Subsequently, your federal criminal defense attorney is allowed to present your case, including advising you on testifying or exercising your right to remain silent.

It is your right and your right alone to testify or not testify. The decision cannot be used against you by the prosecution or the jury.

This decision among many others should be decided with advice of experienced federal criminal defense counsel.

In addition to deciding the law and evidence admissible at trial, the federal judge will decide the law to instruct the jury on; the jury instructions. This decision will dictate what the jury must find in order to decide the verdict, and how to consider the evidence. Your federal criminal defense attorney's ability to argue jury instructions plays a large role in the success of your case.

Closing argument is the last chance for your federal criminal defense attorney to argue your case and the prosecution's failure to prove your guilt beyond a reasonable doubt. The prosecutor will be able to argue the government's case as well.

The final and most important part of your federal criminal trial is jury deliberation. During deliberations, the jury is charged with reaching a unanimous verdict, the jury must all vote for your guilt or you will not be convicted. Upon a verdict of not guilty, a federal criminal defendant is allowed to go home and go on with their life. However, upon conviction, post-conviction proceedings begin.

What Happens After Trial?

Prior to sentencing or appeal, a federal criminal defendant may file post-trial motions to address errors during the course of trial. One such motion is the Motion for Judgment as a Matter of Law "JMOL"; Rule 50. This motion tests the sufficiency of the prosecution's evidence of a charged crime, and your federal criminal defense attorney must illustrate how there are not genuine, material facts entitling the prosecution to judgment as a matter of law.

Motions to Alter or Amend Judgment; Rule 59(e); is a tool to ask the court to substantively change judgment in the case. Motions for a New Trial, if it is "in the interest of justice" may be granted by the District Court, as well as Motions for judgment of acquittal, or motions to set aside or correct a sentence.

These are a portion of the post-trial motions available to federal criminal defendants. Each have their own implications and set of potential benefits and detriments. The decision to purpose one or more of these motions should be discussed with your federal criminal defense attorney.

Federal Trial Sentencing

Federal Sentencing consists of a very complex analysis, established by Congress, which sets minimum and maximum sentences for many crimes for judges to use in attempting to set a proper sentence. As in state criminal prosecution, Presentence Reports are used along with statements by interested parties to determine the sentence. A large number of aggravating factors and mitigating factors are considered by the judge as well, such as the federal criminal defendant's criminal history, if any; whether any remorse has been expressed by the federal criminal defendant; the nature of the crime committed, and other relevant factors. Your chosen defense attorney again has the opportunity to artfully tell your story and the circumstances of your case that warrant leniency in your sentence.

MILITARY CRIMINAL DEFENSE OVERVIEW

As a Judge Advocate and private military defense attorney, I am tasked with defending Service Members through a wide range of legal processes and procedures that make up our military justice system, including the spectrum of employment law, administrative law, and criminal law.

On one end of the spectrum you have purely employment law issues, which consist of: counseling statements; evaluations – Officer Evaluation Reports or Non-Commissioned Officer Evaluation Reports; and Reprimands. These actions are initiated by a supervisor or commander and can have negative implications on a Soldier's career or finances. Service members have limited due process rights in these proceedings, however, experienced counsel can facilitate crafting and presenting rebuttals, letters of support, and may communicate with your commander's JAG or commander directly on your behalf.

The bulk of the military justice system on active duty and in the reserve context consists of the middle ground, Administrative law. Administrative military justice procedures consist of: removal from promotion lists; reduction in rank; withdrawal of federal recognition; non-judicial punishment, and a variety of other actions, each with its own unique procedure, regulations, and level of due process, which necessitates experienced counsel assisting you through the process you are facing and ensuring your rights are protected.

This broad category of actions can have serious implications; however, none of these actions can result in confinement. You need an advocate on your side, outside of the command structure, to ensure the process you are facing is followed precisely and you are afforded the maximum opportunity to receive the best outcome.

Finally, the criminal justice end of the spectrum, which comes from the state or federal code of military justice, carries penalties consistent with state and federal criminal prosecution. The potential for confinement or imprisonment is in addition to the other negative impacts in military justice, such as continued income, retirement, rank, and hard labor.

Federal service members are held to the Uniform Code of Military Justice ("UCMJ"), found in U.S. Code Title 10. National Guard Soldiers are held to their individual state's code, if they are in a non-federal status. Oklahoma National Guard Soldiers are under the Oklahoma Military Justice Code ("OCMJ"), Oklahoma Statutes title 44. Actions under the UCMJ/OCMJ are the most similar to state and federal criminal procedure and can result in restrictions, confinement including but not limited to prison, and discharge from the armed services.

The law and procedure in military justice actions is distinct from the law and procedure found in civilian criminal courts. First, apprehension, arrest, requires far less in military context than civilian. R.C.M. 302 grounds for apprehension, "exists when there are reasonable grounds to believe that an offense has been or is being committed..." Id. at 302(b)(1)(c). Further, the RCM discussion for section 302 states that "reasonable grounds" means that there must the kind of reliable information that a reasonable, prudent person would rely on, which makes it more likely than not that something is true..."

This standard is comparable to civil actions, and far lower than what is necessary to arrest in a civilian context; probable cause. Additionally, military prosecution, Convening Authorities ("CA"), are held to a much lower standard than civilian courts in deciding whether to pursue charges.

In United States v. Boyce, 76 M.J. 242, 250 (C.A.A.F. 2017), the Court held a CA can refer charges for little, if any, reason under the R.C.M. 601(d)(1) based on the military's "reasonable grounds" standard, including that the determination to prosecute may be "based on hearsay in whole or in part." The CA may consider information from "any source and shall not be limited to the information reviewed by any previous authority..." Id. at 601(d)(1).

The legal conclusion is simple, in military criminal justice reasonable grounds that you committed some wrongdoing is sufficient to refer charges to trial. When faced with a potential action in the spectrum of military justice, it is important to have an advocate, who understands the procedures and issues you are facing.

MILITARY ADMINISTRATIVE PROCEEDINGS OVERVIEW

As an enlisted service member in any branch of the military, there are multitude of potential basis for separation you may face. Being separated from the military and the characterization of service you receive when separated from the military can and will have lasting effects on your employment opportunities, retirement and Department of Veterans Affairs benefits, finances, and potentially confinement.

All this makes it essential that you obtain competent and zealous representation as soon as you are aware you are facing potential criminal charges or separation. Each branch of the military has regulations that dictate the basis, procedure, and due process involved for each type of separation, from Court-Martial to retirement. This discussion will focus on Army Regulations for simplicity, but it is important to note the listed processes may not mirror your branch of service.

Army Regulation 635-200, Active Duty Enlisted Administrative Separations, is the basis for separating enlisted soldiers from the Army. These processes may be Command or soldier driven. The following grounds for separation, "Chapters", are the most common in the Army.

Army Chapter Separations

"Chapter 5" – For the Convenience of the Government:

Chapter 5 separations can be voluntary or involuntary, and soldiers must be familiar with their due process rights. The grounds for Chapter 5 discharges are limitless, including, but not limited to: Surviving Sons and Daughters (para. 5-4); Parenting issues (para. 5-8); Unlawful Aliens (para. 5-10); Failure to Qualify Medically (para. 5-12); Personality Disorder (para. 5-13); Concealment of Arrest Record (para. 5-14); and Further Education (para. 5-16).

In involuntary separation proceedings, under Chapter 5, experienced military defense counsel will ensure the government meets their burden, and that your statement or rebuttal presents the relevant issues in the best light possible for your defense. In voluntary separations, experienced military defense counsel will ensure proper procedures are followed and that you receive your maximum benefits.

"Chapter 6" – Dependency & Hardship:

Chapter 6 separations are for the convenience of the government, and is an avenue to seek separation due to a Dependency or Hardship issue in the soldier's personal life. Upon meeting the criteria, evidence and procedures established in paragraphs 6-4 through 6-8, a soldier is entitled to separation; however, complying with the stringent requirements and convincing command of this right requires retaining experienced military defense counsel to advocate for your requested separation.

"Chapter 7" – Defective Enlistment, Reenlistment and Extensions:

This chapter concerns soldiers enlisted before the age of 18. Families with children who enlisted before reaching 18 years of age should obtain experienced counsel to assist them in working through this process.

"Chapter 8" – Voluntary Separation for Pregnancy:

This chapter concerns voluntary separation due to pregnancy; however, it can result in a characterization of service and it is important to have military counsel assist you throughout the process.

"Chapter 9" – Alcohol and Drug Abuse Rehabilitation Failure:

Soldiers with six or more years of active and reserve service are entitled to a board. Soldiers with less time are entitled to submit a written rebuttal to the separation proceeding. It is crucial to retain experienced military defense counsel to assist in preparing and presenting your hearing or rebuttal under chapter nine.

"Chapter 11" – Entry Level Performance and Conduct:

The grounds for this type of separation is unsatisfactory performance or minor disciplinary infractions. This type of discharge is only applicable within your first 180 days of active duty service. The grounds or criteria for this separation are found in paragraph 11-2, as follows: Unsatisfactory performance and/or conduct evidenced by (a) inability; (b) lack of reasonable effort; (c) failure to adapt to military environment; (d) minor disciplinary infractions.

You are entitled to counsel and the opportunity to respond or rebut your separation during this process. You should seek experienced military defense counsel to assist you in your response and advocating on your behalf with your command.

"Chapter 13" - Unsatisfactory Performance:

The grounds for this type of separation is simply unsatisfactory performance, just like the title; however, the criteria in paragraph 13-2: an untrainable soldier or a disruptive influence, can be rebutted. You should seek experienced military defense counsel to assist you in your response and advocating on your behalf with your command.

"Chapter 14" - Misconduct:

The grounds for a misconduct discharge are broad and include a conviction by a civil or foreign court as well as patterns of misconduct. The criteria is found at paragraph 14-12 as states: "Discreditable conduct and conduct prejudicial to good order and discipline including conduct violating the accepted standards of personal conduct found in the UCMJ, Army regulations, the civil law, and time-honored customs and traditions of the Army."

You are entitled to counsel and the opportunity to respond or rebut your separation during this process. You should seek experienced military defense counsel to assist you in your response and advocate on your behalf with your command.

"Chapter 10" - Discharge in Lieu of Trial by Courts-Martial:

An avenue soldiers may exercise to resolve a military criminal matter or punitive matter pending in a court-martial, following preferral or referral of charges. Soldiers may request a Chapter 10 Discharge in Lieu of Trial by Courts-Martial, but should obtain representation to assist in the process to ensure their rights are protected and they understand the forfeiture they are offering the government.

The criteria for a Chapter 10, found at paragraph 10-1, only require the service member is pending a Courts-Martial with an offense punishable by a Bad Conduct Discharge ("BCD") or Dishonorable Discharge. It is essential to have experienced counsel in a situation where a service member is considering offering a Chapter 10 discharge, as he/she is facing a Court-Martial proceeding with prison/confinement; financial consequences, future employment considerations, and other issues are on the line.

Consequences Of Separation From The Military

You are entitled to a defense, and you need one, if you are facing an involuntary separation or you are seeking a voluntary separation. Cannon Law Firm can assist you and ensure your rights are protected and the proper procedure is followed in your military justice case. You are entitled to the following at the very least in any separation action:

- Notice of the specific separation action
- Basis of your separation action

- Notice of the least favorable characterization of discharge you can receive
- Notice of the characterization of service your commander recommends
- Right to speak to a military defense attorney
- Right to submit matters and evidence on your behalf
- Right to request a Board, and counsel to represent you in a number of these Chapters
- Right to an Administrative Board, if your commander is recommending an Other than Honorable ("OTH"); Bad Conduct Discharge ("BCD"); or Dishonorable Discharge
- Right to an Administrative Board, if you have more than 6 years of qualifying service
- Right to submit a conditional waiver (military justice version of an offer/plea agreement)
- Right to request witnesses on your behalf

Know Your Rights Before Separation Or Other Military Justice Action

It is important to know your rights and retain an experienced military defense attorney if facing any military justice action, including separation proceedings, whether enlisted or commissioned. The fact your command has initiated a military justice action or separation does not mean you are guilty, nor does it mean you will be separated. You have rights and your attorney will ensure they are protected.

Choose An Experienced Military Criminal Defense Lawyer

Cannon Law Firm will do everything possible to defend your service, your freedom and your future. You have the right to the presumption of innocence, and representation by the best military criminal defense attorney you can find.

DRUG CRIMES IN OKLAHOMA

Drug crimes are taken seriously by prosecutors in Oklahoma, from simple possession to complex drug trafficking and racketeering schemes. A large percentage of state prisoners in Oklahoma are incarcerated based on drug crimes. Facing drug charges can affect multiple aspects of your life, including your freedom, finances, and your future.

Drug charges carry more than a potential prison sentence; they potentially carry heavy fines, difficult probation, and a complex counseling and or treatment program. Unfortunately, the harshest punishment in drug cases is often the lasting effect on your record and career. A conviction may appear on background checks and make it difficult to obtain employment, loans, and professional licenses. It is essential to obtain quality legal representation from an Oklahoma drug crime defense attorney who has helped hundreds of clients obtain the best possible outcome in their particular circumstance.

You need an experienced attorney who will fight for you, if you have been arrested, charged, or you are being investigated. Drug charges in Oklahoma come in many forms, and each case and or charge require a different approach. All the charges can be found in Title 63 of the Oklahoma Statutes.

- Possession, Controlled Dangerous Substance

- Possession, Controlled Dangerous Substance within 1000 feet of a school or park
- Possession with Intent to Distribute
- Possession, Controlled Dangerous Substance Proceeds
- Trafficking, Controlled Dangerous Substances
- Aggravated Trafficking, Controlled Dangerous Substance
- Maintaining a Dwelling where Possession with the Intent to Manufacture
- Possession with Intent to Distribute Imitation Controlled Dangerous Substance
- Conspiracy to Distribute a Controlled Dangerous Substance

Prior to July of 2017, you would be charged with a felony for possession even a very small amount of certain controlled substances. This was true, even with no prior criminal record. However, after this update to drug laws in Oklahoma, simple possession in Oklahoma became a misdemeanor offense, even if you have prior felony charges or convictions for possession of drugs. Possession now carries up to one year in jail and up to a $1,000 fine for first time offenders.

Possession with Intent to Distribute drugs is still a felony, which carries prison time. Whenever an individual is arrested with an amount of drugs law enforcement believes is more than an amount for personal use and or the person has drug paraphernalia, such as multiple baggies, a scale, or other items that indicate dividing or selling drugs; a person will likely be arrested and charged with felony possession with intent to distribute. Being charged with this crime is very serious, and in addition to carrying large fines and collateral consequences, a defendant is faced with the potential of up to life in prison even on a first offense.

A commonly known term in drug crimes is trafficking drugs; however, the distinction between drug trafficking and distribution is often unclear to my clients. The primary difference between the two is, in trafficking cases the amount, or weight, of drugs is higher.

Distribution

No minimum or maximum amounts are set forth in Oklahoma statutes to quantify distribution of drugs. Rather, it is primarily a totality of the circumstances analysis, meaning if a prosecutor believes you may be sharing drugs or selling drugs then you will be charged with distribution.

Trafficking

Drug trafficking in Oklahoma, as is the case in most states, is dependent upon a threshold or minimum amount or weight of drugs that law enforcement believes can be tied directly to a single defendant. The volume amounting to Trafficking for some of the most common drugs is as follows:

- Marijuana: 25 pounds
- Methamphetamine: 20 ounces
- Cocaine: 28 grams
- Heroin: 10 grams

- Ecstasy or MDMA: 10 grams or 30 pills
- Hydrocodone: 3,750 grams
- Oxycodone: 400 grams
- Morphine: 1,000 grams
- LSD or Acid: 1 gram
- Benzodiazepine: 500 grams

The exact penalty for drug trafficking and distribution depends on the specific type of drug and amount or volume of drugs involved. The penalty can include up to life in prison for these offenses and up to half-a-million dollar fine.

Drug Schedules in the United States

All drugs, whether inherently legal or illegal, fall under one of five Drug Schedules determined by the Drug Enforcement Agency of the United States, the DEA. This list includes the most dangerous illegal drugs all the way down to common prescription medicine.

Schedule I: this category of drugs has no "federally accepted" medicinal purpose and has the highest potential for drug abuse. This category includes drugs such as: marijuana, heroin, LSD (acid), MDMA (ecstasy), mushrooms, and many more.

Schedule II: this category of drugs has minimal accepted medical purposes and those that are accepted are highly regulated due to the highly likelihood for abuse of this schedule of drugs, including: cocaine, morphine, codeine, other opioids, other painkillers, and opium.

Schedule III: this category is the middle ground with a moderate risk of abuse and more commonly accepted medical purposes than Schedule II. Some of the drugs falling under Schedule III are hormones, narcotic compounds, anabolic steroids, and barbiturates.

Schedule IV: this category includes drugs with very common medical purposes with little risk of abuse, such as Ambien, Ephedrine, Klonopin, Valium, and Xanax.

Schedule V: this category is reserved for drugs, which the DEA believes has very little likelihood of abuse, i.e. these drugs are not stimulants or depressants and contain a low amounts of narcotics.

Another often overlooked and widely contested area of drug defense is possession of drug proceeds. Anything law enforcement believes is purchased from the sale of drugs can be categorized as drug proceeds, including but not limited to the following: homes, cars, motorcycles, televisions, electronics, drug paraphernalia, items used in the creation or storage of drugs, equipment used in the cultivation, production, or transportation of drugs, as well as your money, whether cash or in a bank account.

In order to be charged and convicted of possession of drug proceeds, the prosecution must prove a connection between the item of value and drugs. Specifically, knowingly acquiring, receiving goods, or derived from a violation of the Dangerous Substance Act. These charges are subject to overreach and an experienced defense attorney can hold the government to its burden and help you.

As discussed in previous chapters, the prospect of obtaining a positive result in criminal cases involving drug charges is greatly increased with hiring criminal defense counsel with experience defending drug cases. Additionally, participating in the most appropriate treatment or rehabilitation program, while your case is pending, will increase the likelihood of obtaining a positive outcome in your case. There are a variety of diversion options and treatment programs available for drug offenses. Please see Chapter 22 Diversion Programs in Oklahoma for more information.

There are a variety of diversion options and treatment programs available for drug offenses. Please see Chapter 22 Diversion Programs in Oklahoma for more information. The outcome of your case can greatly improve by hiring the right drug crime defense attorney. Your attorney's experience and knowledge surrounding these issues and others concerning drug offenses is a very important piece to your future.

DRIVING UNDER THE INFLUENCE

Facing a Driving While Under the Influence of Alcohol or Drugs: ("DUI"); Driving While Impaired: ("DWI"); or Being in Actual Physical Control while under the Influence: ("APC"), is a daunting obstacle to overcome in Oklahoma.

When charged with a DUI or DWI you are facing the potential of jail time, lost employment opportunities, substantial probation and court costs, as well as the potential loss of your driving privilege; that's right, driving is a privilege not a right.

All this is to say, it is essential that you obtain competent and zealous representation as soon as you are arrested on suspicion of a motor vehicle or other offense involving operating while intoxicated; I.E. DUI, DWI, or APC.

One key reason for quickly retaining counsel in a DUI, DWI, or APC case that is not at issue in other criminal charges, is the very limited time window you have to seek a modified driver's license or a contested hearing with the Department of Public Safety ("DPS") before your license is revoked.

Definitions and Information

This area of criminal defense is one of the most complicated in any jurisdiction. DUI and the surrounding charges, legal principles, and administrative action involving DPS and your driver's license all intertwine into a formula, which you and your counsel must navigate or suffer financial consequences and the loss of your driver's license.

First, the most common term, DUI: the act of operating a vehicle while being over the legal limit for blood alcohol content ("BAC"). In Oklahoma, a BAC of .08 percent or higher constitutes DUI for any driver 21 years of age or older. In Oklahoma, a BAC of .04 percent or higher constitutes a DUI for commercial driver's license, which can amount to one drink within a relatively short period of time for some individuals. Additionally, in Oklahoma, a driver under the age of 21 can be convicted of DUI for a BAC above zero percent.

DUI does not only apply to motor vehicles, cars. It can apply to boats, utility vehicles, all-terrain vehicles ("ATV"), motorcycles, mopeds, heavy machinery/construction equipment, and other conveyances. Additionally, DUI can be constituted by drugs, commonly referred to as DUI-D. Second, APC: the act of being in physical control of a motor vehicle or other conveyance, discussed above, while under the influence of alcohol/drugs. You can be arrested, charged, and convicted of APC for being asleep in a parked car, while intoxicated, if you are on or adjacent to a public road.

However, there are detailed elements, which the prosecution must present in order to obtain a conviction for the charge of APC. It is essential your attorney know and hold the prosecution to these requirements.

Third, Implied Consent, in Oklahoma, as mentioned earlier driving is a privilege, not a right; therefore, all drivers implicitly consent to one of the following tests to determine if a driver is intoxicated: blood test to determine chemical makeup of your blood, i.e. BAC; urinalysis to determine BAC; or a breath test, i.e. breathalyzer to determine the content of your breath, which is alcohol to formulate a BAC. Failure to submit to one of the Oklahoma tests can subject you to harsh penalties related to your driver's license privilege as well as criminal and financial penalties.

Consequences of A DUI Conviction In Oklahoma

A criminal charge and a warrant for arrest, in District or Municipal Court, will follow an arrest for DUI, DWI, or APC. Being convicted of one of these offenses comes with harsh penalties, including, but not limited to the following:

- Loss of your Driver's License or Commercial Driver's License privileges
- Mandatory completion of an alcohol/drug assessment and program ("ADSAC")
- Attendance of a Victim's Impact Panel
- Narcotics Anonymous ("NA") or Alcoholics Anonymous ("AA") meetings
- Jail time
- Community Service

- Ignition control device, installed in any vehicle you operate at your expense
- Personal and professional consequences
- Potential Federal Crime, DUI, APC, or DWI constitutes a federal crime, if the offense occurs on federal land, including Tinker Air Force Base, Ft. Sill, Vance Air Force Base, or any federal land, such as national parks.

Know Your Options, if Charged with a DUI Crime in Oklahoma

It is important to know your rights and retain an Oklahoma criminal defense attorney with experience defending DUI; DWI; and APC cases as soon as possible. Your life and freedom are on the line and you need a defense. Defenses are available in your criminal case and administrative proceeding before DPS, but you need a defense attorney who can use this information to your benefit.

The fact you were arrested and charged with DUI, does not mean you will be convicted. You have rights and your attorney will ensure they are protected. Defenses are available to contest your charges and the tests police conducted; however, an experienced DUI defense attorney is needed to maximize your chance for a successful outcome.

An experienced Oklahoma DUI attorney can reduce the negative impact your case has on your life and may be able to obtain a dismissal. The following are common Constitutional and other legal grounds to be raised by your Oklahoma DUI defense attorney:

Police lacked probable cause to pull you over, a Constitutional requirement prior to seizing a driver;

Police violated other Constitutional Rights: access to counsel; improper questioning; improper search of your vehicle or person. You can learn more about Vehicle stops in this article, which I have published in the Oklahoma Bar Journal.
https://www.okbar.org/wp-content/uploads/2018/06/OBJ2013Aug17-sm.pdf

In an APC case, you may not have legal actual physical control of the vehicle. Most commonly, *the officer failed to follow proper procedure in administering or interpreting the Field Sobriety Test.* https://jpcannonlawfirm.com/dui-lawyer/

The testing device, Breathalyzer or BAC device, was not functioning correctly or not calibrated correctly.

Unfortunately, facing a DUI charge is a very common problem for people in Oklahoma; however, with experienced counsel and application of the laws that protect your rights and the privilege to drive, you will be able to achieve the best possible outcome in a difficult situation.

YOUR DRIVER'S LICENSE AFTER DUI IN OKLAHOMA

The process for recovering your Driver's License or seeking a Modified Driver's License is a complex process with very particular procedures. It is crucial you contact an experienced criminal defense attorney, if you are facing a DUI or the potential to have your license revoked by the Oklahoma Department of Public Safety ("DPS).

Process To Reinstate Driver License

Being arrested for DUI or APC is one of the most terrifying experiences in most people's lives. However, being arrested is only the start of a long and stressful process to not only save your name and career, but your privilege to drive a vehicle in public.

After you have been arrested for DUI or APC and you either (1) test over the legal limit or (2) refuse to submit to a blood or breath test, the arresting officer will serve you with an "Affidavit and Notice of Revocation" and will seize your driver's license on the spot. The Affidavit serves as a temporary driver license, and a notice that the DPS will revoke your driver's license in 30 days. So long as you are a first offender, the temporary license allows you to drive for a month from the date the officer served you the affidavit.

When the 30-day period expires, you may not legally drive, unless your driver's license has been returned by DPS or you have qualified for a modified driver license. However, at the time of your arrest when your license was taken, if your license was not valid or if it was expired, you do not have the option to receive a temporary driver license and will not be allowed to operate a vehicle until you have legally obtained a valid driver's license.

Following your arrest, the officer will ask you to submit to a blood or breath test to measure the amount of alcohol in your blood or breath. If you agree to take the breath test, the officer will send your test results to DPS to determine whether or not there is cause to revoke your driving privilege, or correct not your right to drive, but your privilege. The laboratory will then contact DPS with the test results. If DPS determines your driving privileges should be revoked due to the amount of alcohol in your blood, DPS will send you an **"Order of Revocation"** in the mail. The Order will tell you the exact date your driving privileges will be revoked.

If the arresting officer seized your driver license, you are not allowed to apply for a renewal or a replacement license while your license is in the custody of DPS or a law enforcement officer. Failure to comply with this rule will result in a misdemeanor crime punishable by imprisonment, from a minimum of seven days to a maximum of six months, and/or a fine of up to $500.00. You can however, request a modified driver's license.

If you do not wish to contest the revocation of your driving privileges and merely wish to drive during your revocation period, you have the option to request a modified driver license. When driving privileges are revoked as a result of a driver license revocation or suspension, the person can obtain relief from a lack of driving privileges during the mandatory revocation period if DPS agrees no other adequate means of transportation exists for the person whose driving privileges have been revoked.

Modifications are sometimes permitted for *Implied Consent Revocations* which include breath and blood refusals following a DUI or APC arrest. A modified driver license will replace your original Class D license and allow you to operate a noncommercial motor vehicle so long as the vehicle has an interlock device in the vehicle. In order to get a modified driver's license, you must pay DPS $175.00, in addition to the expenses associated with installing and maintaining the interlock device.

If you wish to request a modified driver's license, you must complete the "**Request for Modified Driver's License**" (Request) form available from DPS—any other type of request will be returned to the sender as non-compliant. The Request can be mailed or hand delivered to DPS. A Modified Driver's License grants you limited driving privilege during the revocation period. Unlike a request for an administrative hearing, you can request a Modified Driver's License even if more than 15 days have expired after receiving the Affidavit.

You can also request a hearing in front of DPS if you disagree with the merits of the potential revocation. Similar to the procedure for requesting a modified driver's license, you must complete a "**Request for Hearing**" form available from DPS.

A Hearing Request, however, differs from the modified driver's license procedure in that there is a very small window of time during which you have the right to request an administrative hearing in front of the DPS. If you fail to request a hearing within the time period provided, your driving privilege will be automatically revoked.

If you submitted to a breath test, you have 15 days from the date you were arrested and served with the Affidavit to request the hearing. If you submitted to a blood test, you must request a hearing by the date specified on the Order of Revocation sent to you by DPS.

An Administrative Hearing in front of DPS is an opportunity for your attorney to present evidence that your driving privileges should not be revoked. Keep in mind, the hearing's only function is to determine whether or not your driving privileges will be revoked by DPS.

However, the determination made at the hearing is completely distinct from your criminal case. It cannot be used to prove innocence or guilt in your criminal case. Once the hearing is complete, your attorney will be sent an order either sustaining or setting aside your revocation. If the revocation is set aside, no further action is required and your driving privileges will be restored in full.

If your revocation is sustained you can appeal the decision to the District Court in the county you were arrested, so long as you comply with the procedural requirements set forth by the Department of Public Safety.

DPS Consequences and Processes

OFFENSE	LENGTH OF SUSPENSION	FEES
DUI	First Revocation- 180 days Second Revocation within the preceding ten years- 1 year or > Third or > Revocations within the preceding ten years- 3 years or longer	Pay $315.00 to DPS
Aggravated DUI	First Revocation- 180 days Second Revocation within the preceding ten years- 1 year or > Third or > Revocations within the preceding ten years- 3 years or longer	Pay $315.00 to DPS
Driving While Impaired	The first suspension is 30 days. The second suspension is six months. The third or subsequent suspension is for 12 months.	Pay $315.00 to DPS
APC	First Revocation- 180 days Second Revocation within the preceding ten years- 1 year or > Third or > Revocations within the preceding ten years- 3 years or longer	Pay $315.00 to DPS

IGNITION INTERLOCK DEVICE DURATION	STATE APPROVED ALCOHOL/DRUG ASSESSMENT
First Revocation- If the person refused to submit to a test, or had a blood or breath alcohol concentration of 0.15 or more =1/12 years after the mandatory period of revocation or until the driving privileges of the person are reinstated, whichever is longer Second Revocation- A period of 4 years following the mandatory period of revocation or until the driving privileges of the person are reinstated, whichever is longer Third or Subsequent Revocation- A period of 5 years following the mandatory period of revocation or until the driving privileges of the person are reinstated, whichever is longer	Must complete all recommendations following the assessment. This may take up to twelve months to complete. Once completed, a completion certificate will be provided to you. You must then provide the certificate to the Driver Compliance Division of DPS

Timely Request to DPS

A timely Request for Hearing will stay the Department's action until completion of the hearing or until you have been granted a Modified Driver's license. When a Request for Hearing is submitted on time, you will be allowed full driving privileges pending resolution of the administrative hearing, or granting the Modified Driver's license.

It is DPS' discretion to grant a request for a Modified Driver's license. You will be notified and asked to complete an "**Information for Modified Driver's License**" form, if granted. Before a Modified Driver's License can be issued, you must pay a $175 modification fee to DPS.

If you think the process and legal issues involved with DPS are complicated, you are correct. The process of seeking to protect your driver's license after a DUI or APC is highly technical and all errors are held against you, not the state. It is important you hire an experienced DUI defense attorney that understands DPS legal procedures and can hold the state to its procedural and legal burdens. Your driver's license is too important to let chance control the outcome.

CRIMINAL CHARGES FOR YOUTH IN OKLAHOMA

It is important to know your rights and retain an Oklahoma juvenile criminal defense attorney with experience defending children and minors, if you or your child/minor family member has been accused or charged with a juvenile crime. Your life and freedom are on the line and you need a defense. In Oklahoma, there are a wide variety of juvenile criminal offenses, and a unique procedure that requires experienced counsel to help you navigate.

Juvenile Criminal Defense

Children and teenagers facing the difficulties of life, school, family, and peer pressure sometimes turn to poor outlets and poor choices, including drugs, alcohol, and crime, when faced with these and other tough circumstances. Cannon Law Firm works every day to ensure our clients' bad choices don't ruin their lives. Young men and women need quality and compassionate defense counsel with experience defending juvenile criminal cases. Choosing the right juvenile criminal defense attorney is a very important decision.

The stakes when a minor child is accused or charged with a crime are very high. A conviction for a violent or serious offense can have consequences that follow them for life, especially, if the child has had prior criminal trouble.

Juvenile criminal prosecution consists of a number of separate processes, which take place at the same time. The most important determination is how the child offender will be charged and tried: delinquent, youthful offender, or adult. Children facing criminal charges in Oklahoma are subject to one of the three proceedings under the Oklahoma "Youthful Offender Act", OKLA. STAT. tit. 10A, Sections 2-5-201 et. al.:

1. Juvenile Delinquent

2. Youthful Offender

3. An Adult

Each category has a different Process and Procedure, which an experienced juvenile criminal defense attorney will know and ensure is respected for the benefit of your case. A Certification Hearing, to determine whether a child will be tried as an adult or not, is crucial to the case, and your chosen juvenile criminal defense attorney's responsibility is to seek "Certification as a child".

Juvenile Delinquent Adjudication

Juvenile delinquent adjudication is the least serious process for a minor. In Oklahoma, minors under the age of eighteen are not convicted for crimes, unless charged and convicted with specific offenses, discussed below. A child or teen with a juvenile delinquent adjudication may spend time in a detention facility, but the records will be sealed and not visible to the public. This is the least serious of the three categories of processes, and is generally reserved for minor offenses by children fifteen years old or younger.

Youthful Offenders

Youthful Offender is the middle ground, between delinquent and adult. However, these proceedings should not be taken lightly. Proceedings under the Oklahoma "Youthful Offender Act", OKLA. STAT. tit. 10A, Sections 2-5-201 et at. are reserved for serious offenses. Upon conviction in a Youthful Offender charge, the juvenile will receive an adult sentence and be treated the same as an adult; however, the person may be released before being transferred to an adult facility.

Juvenile cases have specific time and pleading requirements, which your attorney must meet in order to protect your rights or the rights of a child facing this process. Additionally, experienced criminal defense counsel can seek relief, including dismissal of the case, if the prosecutor fails to follow the Youthful Offender process.

Juvenile criminal defense counsel must seek certification as a juvenile, and certification as a Youthful Offender, by filing the proper paperwork by the required timeline. Failure to do so may waive your right to these proceedings. Being sentenced as a Youthful Offender is not a conviction in the typical sense, unless the child is bridged to custody of, or supervision by, the Department of Corrections. The purpose of these proceedings is twofold: protect the public and rehabilitate youths through the Office of Juvenile Affairs treatment programs.

Youthful Offenders are teens between the age of fifteen and seventeen charged with specific crimes. Allegations of one of the following offenses may result in a child being charged as a Youthful Offender:

- Second Degree Murder
- First Degree Manslaughter
- Shooting with Intent to Kill
- Discharging a Weapon from a Vehicle
- Aggravated Assault and Battery on an Officer
- Assault and Battery with a Deadly Weapon
- Maiming
- Witness Intimidation
- Assault
- Kidnapping
- Armed Robbery & Attempted Armed Robbery
- First Degree Rape & Attempted First Degree Rape
- Rape by Instrumentation & Attempted Rape by Instrumentation
- Second Degree Rape
- Forcible Sodomy
- Lew Molestation

- First Degree Arson & Attempted First Degree Arson
- First Degree Burglary & Attempted First Degree Burglary
- Second Degree Burglary, after two or more adjudications
- Drug Trafficking
- Drug Manufacturing

When Minors Are Charged As Adults

Only in very serious circumstances will a minor be charged as an adult under Oklahoma law, principally Murder in the First Degree. A number of guidelines must be considered in determining whether a child will be tried as an adult or not. The arguments illustrated on the following guidelines by your selected juvenile criminal defense attorney may decide the course of your case.

The Court is required to give the first three (3) factors great weight:

1. Whether the alleged offense was committed in an aggressive, violent, premeditated or willful manner;

2. Whether the offense was against persons and, if personal injury resulted, the degree of personal injury;

3. The record and past history of the accused person, including previous contacts with law enforcement agencies and juvenile or criminal courts, prior periods of probation and commitments to juvenile institutions;

4. The sophistication and maturity of the accused person and the accused person's capability of distinguishing right from wrong as determined by consideration of the accused person's psycho-

logical evaluation, home, environmental situation, emotional attitude and pattern of living;

5. The prospects for adequate protection of the public if the accused person is processed through the youthful offender system or the juvenile system;

6. The reasonable likelihood of rehabilitation of the accused person if the accused is found to have committed the alleged offense, by the use of procedures and facilities currently available to the juvenile court; and

7. Whether the offense occurred while the accused person was escaping or in an escape status from an institution for youthful offenders or juvenile delinquents.

See OKLA. STAT. tit. 10A, Sections 2-5-206(F)(4)

You or your child are entitled to a defense and you need one, if you are facing a juvenile or Youthful Offender charge in Oklahoma. Cannon Law Firm can assist you and ensure your rights are protected. The system can appear biased against an accused child, hiring the right law firm will ensure your or your child's rights are respected from initial investigation through sentencing or trial and everything between. The fact you or your child are charged with a juvenile or Youthful Offender crime in Oklahoma does not mean you or your child will be convicted or sentenced to jail/prison.

PROPERTY CRIMES IN OKLAHOMA

Property crimes occur every single day in large cities at a substantially higher rate than statewide averages. Additionally, prosecutors come down hard on those accused of property crimes based in part of this fact. When charged with a felony or misdemeanor charge involving theft or damage to property, you are facing a wide variety of serious consequences, which are affected by the type of property crime and your criminal record.

Property crimes in Oklahoma, as in other states, involve the destruction of/damage to an object belonging to another person, or the wrongful taking of an object/property belonging to someone else. The list of property crimes in Oklahoma, include, but is not limited to the following:

- Robbery
- Burglary
- Theft
- Grand Theft Auto
- Unauthorized Use of a Motor Vehicle
- Arson
- Vandalism.

Robbery is generally characterized as a violent crime. Police make millions of arrests every year in the United States. In 2010, over 13 million people were arrested in the United States, only 500,000 of these arrests involved violent crime, which means the vast majority of arrests are property crime related, not violent.

Motor Vehicle Theft; there are multiple types of motor vehicle theft, some of which are considered property crimes, such as unauthorized use of a motor vehicle, possession of a stolen vehicle, and joyriding. However, there are also fraudulent forms of vehicle theft and violent crime, such as vehicle theft commonly referred to as "carjacking." Each of these crimes require a specific set of elements and facts to constitute an offense, for which you can be convicted.

Theft crimes; there are a multitude of crimes involving theft. Some theft crimes are violent, such as robbery and first degree burglary; however, the majority are non-violent, such as: grand larceny, possession of stolen property, tax fraud (stealing from the government), embezzlement (federal and or state crime based on amount and involvement of banking system), business fraud, credit fraud, simply burglary, and petit larceny.

Know Your Options, If Charged With Property Crimes In Oklahoma

It is important to know your rights and retain an Oklahoma criminal defense attorney with experience defending property crimes as soon as possible. Your life and freedom are on the line and you need a defense. You are facing substantial penalties, if convicted of a property felony. In addition to your freedom and reputation being on the line, a felony conviction will deprive you of civil rights – owning or being in the presence of a firearm, voting, holding office, employment/housing, and cause difficulty in obtaining a loan or mortgage, and other penalties.

Cannon Law Firm has reached successful outcomes, including the dismissal or reduction of charges, and negotiated agreements, including: probation, reasonable restitution, and diversion programs. In white collar property cases, Cannon Law Firm has successfully defended clients through zealous advocacy, detailed independent investigation, holding witnesses' credibility under a microscope, and ensuring client's rights are protected under the law. You need a fierce advocate to defend your life and freedom, if you have been accused of or believe you are about to be accused or charged with a property crime in Oklahoma.

Our firm will do everything possible to defend your freedom and your future. As a former prosecutor, I know being charged with a crime does not mean you are guilty. You have the right to the presumption of innocence and representation by the best criminal defense attorney you can find. I will investigate the allegations; examine law enforcement conduct; interview all potential witnesses; examine credibility issues with your accusers; identify all potential defenses; and identify every weakness in the prosecution's case.

In the end, there are two main approaches to defending a property crime in Oklahoma: an innocence defense or admission of the act, but defense of the reason you did the specific crime. An innocence defense primarily consists of developing your story and identifying alibis to your location and conduct, if they exist, and attacking the credibility of all eyewitness identification and law enforcement investigation.

In a case where you cannot contest you committed the act, there are several legal and factual defenses available to you: protecting yourself by self-defense, defense of another, which removes your culpability; accident or mistake of fact, i.e. accidental discharge of a firearm shooting someone; mental capacity defenses, such as insanity, lack of the ability to distinguish between right and wrong, or lack of mental capacity; inability to form the requisite intent due to intoxication; and a number of other mitigating and extenuating circumstances. It is important to hire an experienced criminal defense attorney for your property crime defense that has knowledge of property law and defenses available in your case.

ASSAULT & BATTERY CRIMES IN OKLAHOMA

In Oklahoma, there are a wide variety of Assault & Battery Crimes, each with its own legal elements, facts to constitute the crime, and potential punishment.

Prior to explaining the most common Assault & Battery crimes; let's define these two terms:

Assault – the threat to induce physical harm on another person, which must include a physical action, including, but not limited to moving aggressively towards a person.

Battery – the intentional use of force against another person that causes some amount of harm. The amount and source of the force separates many of the different Battery crimes.

Simple Assault: a misdemeanor, which carries potential jail time;

Simple Assault & Battery: a misdemeanor, which requires harmful contact between the defendant and some other party, and carries jail time;

Assault & Battery with a Dangerous Weapon: a felony, which carries prison time without prior felony convictions. The government can charge you with this serious felony after alleging you used an object, which is dangerous, by its use, to induce physical harm to another person. A severe injury is not required in order to be charged with this serious felony charge;

Assault & Battery with a Deadly Weapon: a felony, which potentially carries a very long prison sentence. A deadly weapon is an object meant to inflict harsh bodily injury, such as a gun or a sharp object. However, other objects can be charged as deadly weapons based on the manner they are allegedly used. Any object that can disfigure, break bones, or kill qualifies as a deadly weapon. This is one of the most serious Assault & Battery crimes, and requires the assistance of experienced criminal defense counsel to defend;

Homicide, Manslaughter, and Murder: all felonies, which can carry up to life in prison, or the death penalty for Murder in the First Degree.

The taking of another person's life will potentially expose you to being charged with one of these crimes. It is crucial to have experienced criminal defense counsel that has handled multiple homicide, manslaughter, and murder cases to ensure your rights are protected and you receive the best defense possible.

Being charged with any Assault & Battery crime, especially a felony, can expose you or your loved one to prison time, and or restitution to the victim for; personal issues, medical bills or treatment, and damaged or destroyed property. There also may be lost employment opportunities for years, costly probation fees, and many other costs.

It is important to know your rights and retain an Oklahoma criminal defense attorney with experience defending Murder and Manslaughter cases, as soon as possible. Your life and freedom are on the line and you need a defense.

Facing And Defending Murder Charges In Oklahoma

In Oklahoma there are a wide variety of homicide charges, including: Negligent Homicide, Manslaughter, and Murder. Each has its own elements, criminal intent, and proof requirements.

In Oklahoma, Murder is defined as a homicide with the specific intent to kill. *First Degree Murder* requires proof of malice aforethought, or premeditated intent to kill; which can be formed in an instant under Oklahoma law. *Felony Murder* is charged when someone takes a life or is involved in a crime resulting in the loss of someone's life, sometimes referred to as depraved heart. *Murder in the Second Degree* requires proof of reckless disregard for human life. *Manslaughter in the First and Second Degree* each have their own elements, as well as *Negligent Homicide*.

Self-defense requires proof by the defendant that the homicide was committed for the purpose of protecting your life or the life of another person. Aggravating circumstances increase the guilt or culpability of a defendant during the course of an alleged crime. The prosecution will try to emphasize these factors during the course of a Murder case or Murder trial. Only experienced criminal defense counsel can understand and effectively respond to aggravating circumstances in your case.

Mitigating and extenuating circumstances may be considered and may lessen the charge or penalty a defendant faces. Mitigating circumstances lessen the moral or legal consequences of a crime. Extenuating circumstances excuse or justify conduct. An expert understanding of the law surroundings these principles is critical to your defense. It is crucial to your freedom and defense that you retain a criminal defense attorney with experience defending murder cases and/or other homicide charges, who can develop and tell your story to the prosecution and/or a jury.

WHITE COLLAR CRIME IN OKLAHOMA

Beyond the scope of violent crime and property crime exists an area less frequently discussed but equally important, White Collar Crime. This large, encompassing field of criminal law includes a variety of offenses involving financial crimes for monetary gain of the defendant. With the litany of offenses and potential penalties within the umbrella of White Collar Crime, it is important to know your rights and retain a White Collar criminal defense attorney with experience fighting for clients.

White Collar Crime Investigation

White collar criminal investigations generally begin with a business identifying some act that is fraudulent, or with an allegation of theft. Subsequently, loss prevention or an internal officer is notified and they will contact the suspected employee and seek an admission or confession by intimidation to resolve the matter quickly and discretely; however, these meetings are almost always communicated to law enforcement and result in criminal charges being filed. You should not accept this offer of leniency, whether truthful or a lie, because you will have your opportunity to tell your side of the story later with the assistance of a white collar criminal defense attorney.

Your attorney can work directly with the business to try to resolve the matter without criminal charges being filed, and without your waiving your Constitutional right to remain silent. The loss prevention officer or other employee is not obligated to read you your Miranda rights, and may not be held to the same standard for admissible evidence that law enforcement must meet.

Non-employment based white collar crime is similar; however, it generally originates with law enforcement directly. It is equally important you exercise your right to remain silent, and speak to an experienced white collar defense attorney in this setting. Seemingly small transactions can turn into state or federal prosecution for serious allegations, with local law enforcement referring your matter to federal agencies, such as Homeland Security; the Securities and Exchange Commission ("SEC"); the Internal Revenue Service ("IRS"); the Federal Bureau of Investigation ("FBI"), or other federal agencies.

Types of White Collar Crime

There are two major areas of White Collar Crime: Fraud, and Theft. Fraud is generally an act or scheme of deceit with the intent to deprive or receive an unjustified gain or monetary compensation. Theft is simply the taking of something the person is not entitled to by a variety of actions, not including force or violence, which would be violent crime. The vast majority of Fraud and Theft White Collar Crime is charged as felony offenses in state and federal court.

The effects of being charged or convicted of a white-collar crime can have lifelong consequences. Restitution is the most distinguishing aspect of white collar crime. Restitution is an amount of money determined to make the victim whole or as close to whole as prior to their loss. Further, Oklahoma allows for treble damages (three times the victim's loss) as restitution. An experienced white collar defense attorney can advocate for your case and the amount of restitution you will be obligated to pay, if your case is resolved without going to jury trial. Your attorney can advocate in person or by fighting on your behalf at a hearing to reduce your restitution.

Common White Collar Fraud Crimes:

Forgery

Tax Fraud

Computer Fraud/Scam

Mail Fraud

Credit Card/Securities Fraud

Bank Fraud

White Collar Theft Crimes:

Embezzlement

Extortion

Counterfeiting;

Identify Theft;

Money Laundering

Tax evasion

You or your loved one need experienced criminal defense counsel, if accused or charged with a white-collar crime in Oklahoma. John Cannon is a Fierce Advocate for every client and will use his experience and respected reputation to do everything possible to reach the best possible outcome in your case.

FACTORS IN GOING TO TRIAL ON YOUR CASE

Every case and every client is different. Although most clients have never faced the decision of going to trial and facing prison, an experienced criminal defense attorney has been in the situation with many clients. In a criminal case, the attorney and client have different roles, and although both must work together throughout the process, each have separate responsibilities.

The client decides all substantive issues, including whether or not to go to trial. The attorney may and should advise his/her client about all the pros, cons, and considerations in going to trial, but the decision is the client's and the client's alone. Clients must decide whether to go to trial or enter a plea agreement. It is a difficult decision to make, but with the assistance of experienced attorney every defendant should feel confident in their decision, as they have been able to evaluate all factors in their decision.

The following are some of the most common factors and circumstances in deciding whether to go to trial or enter a plea agreement:

Client accepts guilt: the majority of criminal cases are resolved with a plea agreement. Many of my clients are more than satisfied with the plea agreement our firm is able to obtain in their case, due in part to the work the client does after hiring our firm; see

Chapter Seven. Every plea agreement my clients enter is better than the worst potential outcome and trial.

Client accepts plea offer: sometimes clients accept the plea agreement our firm is able to obtain for them, even if the prosecution's case is not the strongest against the client. The certainty of a favorable plea agreement is often better than the potential for a lengthy prison sentence. Trial is expensive, and the combination of attorney fees, time away from work, time away from family, and the emotional strain is often too much for criminal defendants, which leads many to choose to accept the best plea agreement available in their case.

Collateral Considerations: Some clients face matters outside their criminal case which are very important to them or their family. A criminal defendant that is not a citizen may risk conviction at trial, instead of entering a plea, to avoid the immigration consequences, such as deportation, denial of citizenship, etc. Clients with professional licenses, i.e. Doctors, Realtors, etc. sometimes go to trial to avoid the risk of losing their license and source of income. Additional consequences exists, which apply to specific clients' circumstances.

Lesser offenses: Often, a criminal client will have the option of entering a plea to a lesser charge in exchange for not forcing the prosecutor to prove his/her case at trial. Fewer included offenses sometimes provide a much more favorable outcome for a client, which is reason enough by itself to enter a plea.

Other considerations: there are a number of other factors specific to clients and criminal charges that point towards going to trial or entering a plea; however, they are too numerous to describe here. The important point is to hire an attorney with the experience to recognize those factors and be able to speak intelligently to you about each.

What Will The Offer Be For My First Offense?

The prosecution is not obligated to provide a plea agreement; however, judicial economy and the potential to lose any case at trial dictates the prosecutor in almost all cases makes an offer to resolve the case. The specific offer depends on a number of factors: the charged offense(s); your background; the victim(s); the strength of the prosecution's case; the approach of the prosecuting office; and the experience of your criminal defense attorney, to name a few. There are a variety of potential outcomes in a criminal case; however, other than a dismissal and an apology, a deferred sentence is the best realistic outcome.

A deferred sentence is exactly what is sounds like, the judgment or conviction is deferred, or set off, for a number of months or years. During the delay, you will be required to complete a number of probation requirements; your attorney can and should work to make the conditions easier. Upon successfully completing probation, and staying out of trouble, the case will be dismissed on the date the case was deferred, i.e. if you receive a two-year deferred on January 9th year one, then your deferred sentence would be up on January 8th year three.

In more serious cases, or if you have a criminal record, the best outcome you may seek is a suspended sentence. In a suspended sentence, you receive a felony or misdemeanor conviction; however, your jail or prison sentence is set off for a period of time. Just like the deferred sentence, if you are successful you will not go to jail or prison, but the conviction will remain unless or until you get an expungement. Your case and future depend on hiring an experienced criminal defense attorney to help you decide the best course of action in your case: fight or get the best deal possible. You need a defense attorney with knowledge of the criminal process and defenses available in your case.

STATE COURT CRIMINAL PROBATION

Over ninety-five percent of criminal cases in Oklahoma state courts are resolved without a trial. Seasoned criminal defense counsel can help you seek a dismissal or the best possible resolution of your case. The vast majority of cases are resolved by plea agreement between the prosecution and the Defendant, with the assistance of defense counsel.

Not only is it critical to have competent defense counsel to assist you in reaching the best possible outcome in your case, it is equally important to have experienced criminal defense counsel if you are accused of violating a condition or multiple conditions of your probation.

No proceeding in state court affords a party more protections than a criminal defendant prior to a verdict or entry of a plea agreement. The government has the only burden, period. The government must prove your guilt beyond a reasonable doubt for each element of any offense charged.

However, upon entry of a plea agreement a criminal defendant has limited rights. There are three versions of probation, which a criminal defendant may entered into upon a plea agreement: deferred sentence, suspended sentence, and sentence suspended in part.

A deferred sentence is exactly what it sounds like; the Defendant's sentencing date is deferred or delayed, contingent upon successfully completing and/or complying with all conditions of probation. The Defendant's case will be dismissed and you may seek an expungement of your case, upon successfully reaching the sentencing date without an alleged violation.

A suspended sentence is a conviction with a period of incarceration, in jail or prison; however, the defendant's incarceration or service of their sentence is suspended or postponed, contingent upon successfully completing and/or complying with all conditions of probation. A suspended sentencing is similar to a deferred sentence; however, the defendant is convicted upon entering a plea. The benefit of a suspended sentence is the opportunity to avoid imprisonment/jail time. Upon completing the period of suspension, you cannot be incarcerated for your conviction.

A sentence suspended in part includes incarceration and probation. Upon being released from the period of incarceration/jail time, the defendant will have a suspended period of his/her sentence. Upon reaching the completion of the suspended portion, a defendant cannot be incarcerated for the conviction.

It is imperative you retain experienced criminal defense counsel to protect your rights and advise you of all your options at each phase of the judicial process of Oklahoma state court criminal proceedings. Upon entering probation, you forfeit many of your rights, including the right to a trial by your peers. The prosecutor has the authority to file an Application to Accelerate your sentencing date, on a deferred sentence, and an Application to Revoke your probation, on a suspended sentence, for any violation they believe you have committed.

The process is more administrative than judicial, as the determination as to whether you did or did not violate your probation is a technical determination. At hearing, the prosecutor need only present a limited amount of evidence to meet the low burden of proof that you violated probation, and your deferred sentence can turn into a conviction or you can be sentenced to jail or prison.

It is crucial you obtain experienced counsel, if faced with the harsh reality of contesting a probation violation, to assist you through your options and presenting all the defenses available to you. There are multiple options to consider with an experienced attorney before exercising your right to a contested hearing before a judge, in which you do not know the outcome.

FEDERAL SENTENCING & BEYOND

Federal crimes are enumerated, listed, in United States Code, which contains all the statutory federal law in the United States. The majority of federal crimes are listed in Title 18 United States Code; however, almost every Title of the United States Code contains one or more criminal provisions.

Part of the logic behind the creation of Federal Sentencing Guidelines is uniformity in punishment. The Federal Judiciary, particularly the U.S. Sentencing Commission (discussed in the next section), wanted to correct the injustice of a federal criminal defendant in one federal district receiving a punishment far longer or shorter than a federal criminal defendant charged with the same offense in another part of the county. Although the system still has disparity between Federal Districts, a federal criminal offender in the Western District of Oklahoma will now face a punishment similar to an offender in any District.

Brief History of Federal Sentencing

At the time of enactment, the Federal Sentencing Guidelines were mandatory, meaning federal judges were required to follow the exact framework of the guidelines. However, in 2005 the United States Supreme Court decided United States v. Booker, 543 U.S. 220

(2005), which found the mandatory prong of the Guidelines was not Constitutional.

Although the guidelines results are no longer mandatory, federal judges must perform the calculations in the Federal Sentencing Guidelines and consider the result in determining a federal criminal defendant's sentence. Additionally, federal judges will consider a Presentence Report, which paints a picture of the defendant and the charges.

How Federal Sentencing Guidelines Work

The Federal Sentencing Guidelines are just what they sound like – a guide to sentencing federal criminal offenders. Most, but not all, federal criminal offenses are listed in one of the forty-three (43) "Offense Levels." Additionally, each federal criminal offender is assigned one of the six "Criminal History Categories".

The criminal history categories are based on the offender's criminal history, specifically, the seriousness of their history and how recently the offense occurred. Imaged as a graph; the "Offense Level" is the Y-axis and the "Criminal History Category" is the X-axis. The overlap or intersection of the two axes (Offense level x Criminal History Category) determines the federal criminal offender's range of punishment.

Each "Guideline Range" is separated by six (6) months incarceration or 25 percent (25%), whichever is greater. Judges are now advised, previously required as discussed above, to choose a sentence within the "Guideline Range," unless a factor convinces the federal judge a different sentence is appropriate.

U.S. Sentencing Commission

The Federal sentencing guidelines are written and maintained by an independent federal agency, called the United States Sentencing Commission, a federal agency that is part of the federal judicial branch. The United States Sentencing Commission analyzes criminal sentencing information and consults other branches of government on policies that affect criminal issues.

Offense Levels: Seriousness of Federal Crime

In addition to the sentencing analysis discussed in the last section, forty-three (43) offense seriousness levels exist. You are correct in assuming, the higher the number the more serious the federal offense, i.e. First-Degree Murder has a base offense level of 43 (the highest level). The final offense level is set by taking the "Base Level," explained in the last section and adding or subtracting based on the offense characteristics.

This leads to the next issue; what raises or lowers federal criminal offense levels?

Offense Characteristics: Raising the Offense Level

Specific federal offenses usually carry a number of "Offense Characteristics." The characteristics can increase or decrease the base offense level, which plays a role in the federal sentence received by an offender. The following are some of the most common level adjustments:

Property loss greater than $2,500 – adds one level

Property loss greater than $xx – adds two levels

Property loss greater than $800,000 – adds five levels

Displaying a firearm in a robbery – adds five levels

Discharge of a firearm in a robbery – adds seven levels

i.e. violence and/or great financial loss will increase levels

Now that you are familiar with some of the offense characteristics that increase the base offense level; the next section illustrates "Offense Characteristics" that decrease the base offense level.

Offense Characteristics: Lowering the Offense

Some "Offense Characteristics" lower the offense level. The following characteristics are the most common that lower, decrease, the base offense level:

Substantial Assistance to authorities, discussed below

Participation in an early disposition program

Victim's conduct that significantly contributes to the offense

Lesser harm, discussed below

Federal Sentencing Adjustments

Adjustments are another factor in federal criminal sentencing. They potentially apply to any offense, and will either increase or decrease the offense level. There are three categories of Adjustments: victim-related; offender role; and obstruction of justice. Minimal participation can decrease the base level by four levels. However, obstruction or a crime involving a vulnerable victim will increase the offense level.

Multiple Count: a federal criminal defendant convicted on multiple counts, i.e. more than one federal offense, will receive one "Combined Offense Level" for all the crimes. The guidelines begin with the most serious offense and all other offenses will either increase or not affect the offense level.

Acceptance of Responsibility: the judge may reduce the offense level by two levels for a federal criminal defendant taking or accepting responsibility for the offense. Upon a motion by the prosecution, stating the defendant's early guilty plea avoided U.S. Attorney and court resources, the judge may decrease the offense level by an additional level, if the offense level is at sixteen (16) or higher.

Although federal judges have discretion in applying the downward adjustment, the following factors should be considered:

- Criminal Defendant's truthful admission of participation in crime
- Restitution to the victim before a guilty verdict; and/or
- Entering a guilty plea.

Criminal History: as in state criminal proceedings, the offender's criminal record plays a large role in the guidelines. One of the Six (6) "Criminal History Categories" discussed above will be set based upon the length and how recent previous crimes occurred. Many first-time federal offenders are placed in Criminal History Category One, the lowest category, based on having minimal or no criminal record. Alternatively, criminal offenders with substantial criminal records will be assigned a higher Criminal History Category.

Departures from the Federal Guidelines

Understandably, the Federal Sentencing Guideline point federal defendants are most concerned with is downward departures. This final step in the sentencing analysis is required pursuant to 18 U.S.C. Section 3553(b). The federal judge must determine whether or not aggravating or mitigating, making the offense deserving a lesser punishment, exist that the U.S. Sentencing Commission failed to take into account or failed to give sufficient weight or importance. Federal judges may impose a sentence above or below the guidelines, if he or she determines an aggravating or mitigation circumstance exists and memorializes the reasoning in writing.

Fortunately, federal criminal defendants can appeal, if the federal judge imposes an upward departure. Unfortunately, the U.S. Attorney's Office may appeal, if the federal judge grants a downward departure. The most famous departure is the "Substantial Assistance Departure."

In state court criminal proceedings, cooperation with prosecutors or law enforcement may result in a benefit in your state court criminal proceedings. Likewise, in federal criminal proceedings this downward departure, reduction in prison sentence, may be applied for substantially assisting in the investigation and/or prosecution of another, usually more serious, federal criminal offender.

Federal criminal defense attorneys may not request the "Substantial Assistance Departure," only the federal prosecutor can. However, an experienced federal criminal defense attorney can solidify your receiving such a request by the prosecution, if you provide the proper assistance. Finally, if your federal criminal defense attorney is able to convince the federal judge imposing sentence that following the guidelines would be unreasonable, the federal judge may grant a variance from the guidelines to your benefit. Again, the federal judge must state his or her basis for doing so in writing.

Downward Departure from the Guidelines

An artfully crafted argument by your federal criminal defense attorney may result in additional downward departure. The following are some of the most common downward departure factors:

Victim's Conduct (Section 5K2.10) – when a victim contributes to the significance of a federal criminal offense; a federal judge may depart downward on the sentence below the guidelines to reflect the aggravation by the victim. The federal sentencing judge should consider the following:

The physical characteristics of the victim, in comparison with the defendant;

The victim's conduct, and efforts, if any by the defendant to prevent confrontation;

The danger reasonably perceived by the defendant;

The actual danger to the defendant by the victim;

Any other conduct by the victim affecting the danger presented;

The reasonableness of the defendant's response to the victim's conduct.

Lesser Harm (Section 5k2.11) – when a federal criminal defendant commits a federal crime to avoid a believed greater harm; a federal judge may depart downward on the sentence, if the circumstances diminish the interest in punishing the conduct.

Coercion or Duress (Section 5K2.12) – when a federal criminal defendant commits a federal crime under duress, fear, or blackmail, but it is not a complete defense; a federal judge may depart downward on the sentence.

Diminished capacity (Section 5K2.13) – when a federal criminal defendant commits a federal crime with diminished mental capacity, which contributed to the commission of the offense; a federal judge may depart downward on the sentence. However, voluntary intoxication and other factors may negate this basis for a downward departure.

Voluntary Disclosure (Section 5K2.16) – when a federal criminal defendant admits an offense, which would likely not have been discovered otherwise; a federal judge may depart downward on the sentence.

Aberrant Behavior (Section 5K2.20) – when a federal criminal defendant commits a federal crime that did not involve planning, was of limited duration; and is a deviation from the defendant's otherwise law-abiding life; a federal judge may depart downward on the sentence for policy reasons. However, this does not apply in the case of serious bodily injury; the use of a firearm; or serious drug trafficking.

Punishment Zones

There are four federal sentencing zones, which are set ranges of length of incarceration. A defendant in the lowest of the four zones is eligible for federal probation, i.e. no imprisonment. Further, pursuant to U.S.S.G. Section 5C1.1(c)(3), a federal sentencing judge may create a combination of conditions, including, but not limited to home detention and community confinement. Federal defendants in the third highest zone may receive split sentences, i.e. serve only half of their sentence incarcerated. This topic leads to the consideration of Federal Criminal Probation.

Federal Criminal Probation

The Federal Sentencing Guidelines limit probation to specific circumstances. Probation without any confinement is limited to Zone A, sentencing ranges six months and below, as discussed above. Section 5B1.3 of the Sentencing Guidelines sets out statutorily required and discretionary conditions. The mandatory conditions include:

- Not committing any crimes, including possessing illegal drugs
- Perform community service and make restitution in felonies
- Submit to drug testing, unless suspended by the federal judge
- Keep the court informed of any change in financial circumstances

- Comply with sex offender registration, if applicable
- Computer limitations by sex offenders, if applicable
- Submit to DNA testing

Forms of Confinement

The Federal Sentencing Guidelines list four (4) forms of confinement, which may be imposed as part of probation. 1) community confinement; 2) home detention; 3) shock incarceration; and 4) intermittent confinement.

Community confinement includes circumstances such as a halfway house or rehabilitation center. Home detention, as implied, is supervision from home with the ability to go to work, school, community service work, or out for personal needs. Intermittent confinement is periods of being in custody and out of custody. Shock incarceration is a boot camp, which was discontinued years ago.

In order to facilitate re-entry to the community, federal courts impose supervised release after confinement. Unless statutorily required, federal judges have discretion to waive supervised release. Chapter Seven (7) of the Federal Sentencing Guidelines lays out the penalty for violating the conditions of probation or supervised release, which may include incarceration.

Federal criminal sentencing, and the Federal Sentencing Guidelines, are a highly technical area of criminal law. Federal judges strictly enforce the fast paced and detailed procedures. Federal prosecutors are hard-lined, highly experienced trial attorneys. Your chosen federal criminal defense attorney must be experienced with federal criminal procedure and be a skilled advocate.

In order to intelligently decide the multiple issues you will face during the course of your federal criminal prosecution, you need an experienced and Fierce Advocate. You should contact an experienced federal criminal defense attorney as early as possible in your federal criminal prosecution. It is my hope this page has educated you on major issues in Federal Sentencing Guidelines.

CONSEQUENCES OF A CONVICTION

Being convicted of a felony in Oklahoma is one of the most serious consequences one can face, especially with the collateral consequences that come from a felony conviction. The most well known consequence of a felony conviction is obvious, incarceration, which can consist of a year or less time in a county jail, or up to life in prison.

Misdemeanors are less serious crimes, which carry no more than a year in jail. Felony crimes have a broad range of punishment, from a short prison sentence all the way to life in prison, or even the death penalty for capital murder. Substantial fines and restitution, to make victims whole, can be imposed in felony cases in addition to the length of time one can be sentenced to prison for felony crimes. The fines imposed in felony cases are potentially far greater than one-thousand dollars.

The punishment with the longest lasting effect in most felony cases is the collateral consequences; the negative effects not directly related to the sentence passed down or as part of a felony plea agreement. These collateral consequences, the third type of punishment in a felony conviction, cause the denial of rights and privileges afforded to citizens without a felony conviction. Some, but not all, of these consequences are the following:

- Loss of driving privileges for a period of time;
- Denial of Possessing a liquor store license;
- Loss of the Right to Vote
- Loss of the Right to Possess a Firearm
- Loss of the ability to serve in the Armed Services: Army, Navy, Air Force, Marines, Coast Guard, and Reserve Forces
- Loss of the following employment opportunities:
    - Licensed Attorney
    - Medical Careers: medical doctor, M.D.; dentistry; D.O.; chiropractic medicine; veterinary medicine; nursing; pharmacology; psychology; physical therapy; occupational therapy; and others
    - Accountant
    - Architect
    - Counseling: Marriage; Mental Health; Family; and others;
    - Licensed Realtor or real estate appraiser
    - Law Enforcement: FBI, CIA, Highway Patrol, Police, Sheriff, etc.
    - Licensed Pawnbroker
    - Bail Bondsman
    - Court Reporter

This list is extensive, but not completely exhaustive of the rights, privileges, and opportunities forfeited upon becoming a convicted felon. This list is focused on the consequences of a felony conviction on rights and privileges under Oklahoma law; however, there are consequences under federal law, local ordinances, and administrative consequences, which are not listed here.

A felony accusation is a very serious circumstance to face; however, a felony conviction may follow you and your family the rest of your life. When facing a felony, you have limited opportunities to avoid the long-lasting effects of a felony conviction: enter a plea agreement to avoid a felony offense, fight your case with the assistance of an experienced criminal defense attorney, or seek redress through an appeal.

The decision on how to approach a felony accusation or felony charge is a very important decision. You have the right to competent criminal defense counsel; use it. Hiring the right Oklahoma criminal defense attorney with the experience necessary to assist you through these difficult decisions will be an invaluable investment. You need a Fierce Advocate to protect your rights, your liberty, and your privileges.

DIVERSION PROGRAMS IN OKLAHOMA

We have discussed a variety of topics to this point, but one of the most important topics is alternatives to prison, also known as **Diversion Programs**. There are a number of diversion programs in state criminal courts across Oklahoma. Some of these programs are under the District Attorney's power of deferred prosecution.

In deferred prosecution, the District Attorney dismisses your criminal case upon your acceptance into an applicable diversion program. Generally, you will sign a contract agreeing to participate in the diversion program, and advising you that if you are unsuccessful in the diversion program – including being charged with a new crime – that your criminal case will be refiled and you will be dismissed from the diversion program.

Some Veteran's diversion programs fall under deferred prosecution, including in Oklahoma County. The majority of diversion programs in Oklahoma are based on entering a plea to your criminal charges prior to being admitted or accepted into the specific diversion program. When a criminal defendant enters the majority of diversion programs, a contract is signed that includes the benefit of participation in the program, including: your charges being dismissed upon successful completion, not serving jail or prison time, and receiving/participating in treatment options.

In the unfortunate event a criminal defendant fails one of these diversion programs, he or she will be sentenced based on the contract signed prior to entering the program, and may be sent to jail or even prison. Diversion programs are run by individual counties, which means each of the 77 counties in Oklahoma have their own procedure for application, admission, and successful completion of the programs. Your criminal defense attorney can assist you in applying for and entering into Oklahoma Diversion Programs in your county.

Although failure in either type of diversion program described above may result in being incarcerated, the majority of participants in these programs would be facing jury trial or prison if they did not agree to participate in these programs. Successful completion in almost any diversion program results in the case being dismissed.

Please see a detailed explanation of the most common diversion programs in Oklahoma below:

Veterans Diversion Program

Veteran Diversion Programs, including the Oklahoma County Veteran's Program, are only available to service members who currently or previously served in the United States military. This diversion program is intended to prevent Veterans from serving jail or prison time, while receiving treatment and regiment. Veteran diversion programs are one of the few programs that accept violent offenders.

The service record of every potential participant must be collected and reviewed prior to admission into any veteran diversion programs. This is usually accomplished by the program submitting a DD-214 request to the Department of Veterans' Affairs. Upon service verification, the participant will attend formation for the veteran program; participate in treatment; and participate in job counseling.

All veteran diversion programs aim to reestablish order, mental health, address substance abuse issues, and assist veterans' return to productive lives. You should discuss this diversion option with your criminal defense attorney, if you have served in the United States military, including the National Guard, and you are facing criminal charges in Oklahoma.

DUI/Drug Court

Drug Courts and DUI Courts are the most common diversion programs in Oklahoma. The authority for Drug Court and DUI Court is found at OKLA. STAT. tit. 22 Section 471 et seq. These are comprehensive treatment programs intended to divert individuals away from prison or jail, while helping them to obtain abstinence from alcohol or drugs and treatment to address the issues they are facing. Participation in these programs is voluntary, and includes drug tests, court appearances, treatment, counseling, and job requirements. At least 73 of the 77 counties in Oklahoma offer drug court diversion programs.

The benefits of participating in diversion is obvious, eventual dismissal of your case; however, the consequences are equally apparent. Failure of DUI/Drug Court will result in incarceration. It is important to ensure you understand the terms of your DUI Court or Drug Court contract, because it will lay out the sentence you will receive if you do not successfully complete the program.

Although the goal of these diversion programs is abstinence from drug/alcohol use, program staff and judges understand abstinence is a process and these diversion programs allow for mistakes, with consequences, prior to being kicked out of the program and being sent to jail. You should discuss this diversion option with your criminal defense attorney, if you are facing a DUI or Drug charge in Oklahoma.

Mental Health Court

Mental health issues play a role in the lives of a large percentage of Oklahomans. It is estimated that fifty-five percent (55%) of all Oklahoma offenders have a history or currently suffer symptoms of poor mental health, which does not include the thousands of offenders without documented mental health issues. Oklahoma criminal courts have slowly attempted to respond to this recently identified trend by forming Mental Health Courts.

Treatment for mental health works. At least fourteen counties out of the seventy-seven counties in Oklahoma operate Mental Health Courts. Mental Health Courts are a diversion program based on the Drug Court diversion program model: treatment, counseling, employment or seeking disability resources, and court appearances. Successful completion of Mental Health Court results in your case being dismissed; however, failure will result in jail or prison time.

You should discuss this diversion option with your criminal defense attorney, if you or your loved one who is facing criminal charges suffers from a mental health diagnosis or mental health issue in Oklahoma.

Re-Merge

ReMerge is a comprehensive, evidence-based female diversion program designed to transform pregnant women and mothers facing incarceration into productive citizens.

- ReMerge Oklahoma Mission Statement

ReMerge is a female diversion program for mothers and pregnant women facing prison in Oklahoma. This diversion program works with the Department of Corrections & Department of Mental Health and Substance Abuse Services to find treatment and diversion options for women facing prison. ReMerge, similar to Drug Court, uses treatment to address mental health, behavior health, substance abuse, trauma, and poverty.

Upon successful completion of ReMerge, the participant's felony is dismissed, they are employed, they have housing, and a treatment plan to go forward. ReMerge's comprehensive plan boasts a five percent (5%) recidivism rate, which means only five-percent of graduates re-offend. You should discuss this diversion option with your criminal defense attorney, if you or your loved one potentially qualify for ReMerge in Oklahoma.

Delayed Sentencing for Young Adults

The Delayed Sentencing Program for Young Adults, or Regimented Inmate Discipline Program "RID", is a boot camp style program for criminal defendants between the age of eighteen (18) and twenty-one (21). Individuals must enter a plea before their twenty-second (22nd) birthday to participate in the program, and cannot be charged with any of the specific serious violent felonies listed in OKLA. STAT. tit. 22 Section 996.1.

RID has an in-custody option and an out-of-custody option. After a criminal defendant enters a plea; they will participate in the regimented program for a period between six months and a year. Upon completion of the program, a report is generated that details how the defendant performed. Poor performance or failure of RID can result in a felony conviction or even prison time, while successful completion can result in probation, including a deferred sentence. The defendant's case will be dismissed upon successful completion of a deferred sentence. You should discuss this diversion option with your criminal defense attorney, if you or your loved one are facing criminal charges in Oklahoma and you are under the age of twenty-two.

Community Sentencing

Oklahoma County Community Sentencing is a court ordered diversion program designed to assist individuals by providing supervision, treatment services, personal development, and employment assistance.

– *Mission Statement*

Oklahoma Community Sentencing Act, OKLA. STAT. tit. 22 Section 988.1 et seq. is an alternative to prison for criminal defendants with a prior felony conviction or multiple felony convictions, even some violent crime convictions.

The first step in determining program eligibility is an assessment; the Level of Services Inventory ("LSI") assessment, which gives the defendant's criminal defense attorney, the prosecutor, and the judge insight or a forecast of the likelihood of success for the individual.

Those that do not fall within the qualifying score +19, may be admitted with approval of the applicable District Attorney's office. Although successful completion of Community Sentencing will not result in dismissal of charges; it will result in not going to prison. You should discuss this prison diversion option with your criminal defense attorney, if you or your loved one has one or more felony convictions and is facing new felony charges in Oklahoma.

Alternative Programs for Youth

Juvenile Justice affords greater opportunity to avoid criminal charges, conviction, and incarceration than any other group of criminal defendants in Oklahoma.

The First-Time Offender Program exists to help youth avoid criminal charges. This program, like most, is run by individual counties. **The Skills Education Program** "SEP" exists in Oklahoma County. The SEP is a sixteen-hour course, in which an individual youth and his or her parent work to develop proper responses to anger and conflict. Eligibility for this program requires one of the following: 1) behavior exhibited at school or home that concerns parents or teachers; or 2) a youth that is arrested for a first-time criminal offense.

After a criminal allegation is made against a juvenile, but before charges are filed, a youth may enter into other diversion programs by agreement with the District Attorney's Office through coordinating with the juvenile intake officer in the **Intake and Diversion Services Unit** or the **Community Intervention Center** "CIC".

All three of these options connect youths and their family with services to find better responses to controversy. You should discuss these youth diversion options with your criminal defense attorney, if you or your loved one has youthful criminal allegations or charges in Oklahoma.

CAN I HELP MY ATTORNEY WITH MY CASE?

Yes, you can help your attorney. There are many things you can do throughout the process of your case to help your criminal defense attorney defend you. The biggest and sometimes hardest step is to listen to and trust your selected counsel. You must use due diligence in selecting your criminal defense attorney; for one, so that you can be confident in following their advice.

What Can I Do To Fight My Case Between Court Dates?

Many clients rightfully want to do everything they can to help their cause between court dates. I appreciate and encourage clients to be proactive, with the disclaimer you should only do things for your case that you have consulted with your criminal defense attorney about previously.

Counseling: After consulting with your criminal defense attorney, seeking counseling is potentially a positive step to take to help your case. Counseling for an issue identifiable in your case or personal life can be of great benefit, such as: substance abuse, alcohol abuse, mental health, emotional health issues. Additionally, if you are seeking to resolve your case with a plea agreement, counseling may be a condition of probation, which you get out of the way by completing while your case is pending.

Prosecutors and judges look very favorably on defendants that take steps to address concerns or to simply better themselves. Taking steps to address an issue you or your attorney identify cannot be used against you in court. It is considered a remedial measure to address a concern and is not admissible to prove guilt.

Community Service: After consulting with your criminal defense attorney, completing community service (working for free!) may be beneficial to your case. Again, prosecutors and judges look favorably upon defendants that try to help out in their community. Further, community service will likely be a condition of probation and you can complete this condition, while your case is pending.

Volunteering your time and energy to a good cause, such as a shelter, food bank, or non-profit organization, if you have time outside of work or school, is looked highly upon by prosecutors and judges alike. Volunteering helps illustrate an important narrative of caring about your community and your dedication to getting past the current situation.

Alcoholics Anonymous & Narcotics Anonymous: similar to counseling, attending NA or AA meetings can not only have a positive effect on your life, but a positive effect on your case. Your criminal defense attorney does not have to disclose to the prosecutor that you are attending these meetings, but it is a useful tool for your attorney to be able to reference the good work you are doing.

Complete tasks: An experienced criminal defense attorney, in the right circumstance, will give you tasks to complete while your case is pending. Upon consulting with your attorney, you may be tasked to write a statement, take photographs of a location, get contact information for witnesses (that are not victims or prosecution witnesses), and many other potential tasks. It is important to speak to your attorney before investigating your case, as discussed previously. You should take an active role in your case, as long as you are on the same page as your attorney.

Biography: Your attorney can only articulate your life story if he or she knows it. Every client that hires Cannon Law Firm is asked to put together an autobiography of the good things and the hard things that have happened in their life. It does not have to be a long story, just a page or two, but part of your criminal defense attorney's job is to tell the human side of your story, which should soften the only story the prosecutor knows.

You can collect photographs for your attorney of different accomplishments or highlights of your life. In one case, my client's photographs of before and after suffering from methamphetamine use resulted in the prosecution agreeing to his being placed on probation with treatment as opposed to going to prison for many years. Stories matter in criminal defense, and no one can help your attorney tell your story better than you.

What Can I Do to Prepare My Case For Sentencing?

In Oklahoma, before any sentencing hearing you are entitled to and should exercise the right to a Pre-Sentence Investigation ("PSI"). You should prepare for this part of the process just as you have throughout your case, with continued communication between you and your attorney, and preparing what to say and how to say it.

As discussed in Chapter Thirteen, obtaining substance abuse counseling, treatment, or even inpatient rehabilitation will not only be good for your health if you have a substance abuse issue, it is vital to improve how the prosecutor and judge perceive you. Clients with substance abuse charges may receive a better offer or plea bargain in their case by simply obtaining counseling or treatment.

Paying restitution for property crimes or theft, prior to sentencing in your case, will also greatly improve how the sentencing judge and prosecutor see you and your case. Understand, you should not and in some circumstances, cannot directly provide restitution to the victim. You may however work with your attorney to present a proposal to the prosecutor to repay all or a portion of the requested restitution. Keep in mind restitution may be ordered as treble damages in criminal cases in Oklahoma, meaning you could be ordered to pay three times the requested restitution by a judge.

All of these actions are steps towards "making the victim whole" whether the victim is an individual or the state as a whole. The judge and prosecutor must consider your steps in making the victim whole prior to setting your sentence. I work with each client to draft a statement for sentencing, if they plan to enter a guilty plea. The statement is your opportunity to differentiate yourself from every other case on the judge's docket and the prosecutor's desk. Storytelling is alive and well in criminal defense. Your ability to tell your story, with the guidance of an experienced criminal defense attorney, is vital to reaching the best possible outcome in your case. Creating a plan with your attorney and sticking to it is key in this arena.

Do I Simply Have to Stay Out Of Trouble On Probation?

No, probation in some respects can be more difficult than a jail or prison sentence. Often, probation comes with multiple terms, costs, and expectations that must be met in order to not fail and receive jail time or worse. You can be sentenced to prison for the entire length of your suspended sentence for violating probation. You can be sentenced to prison for the maximum sentence on your charge for violating probation on a deferred sentence. All that is to say, you are far from out of the woods of the criminal justice system after entering a plea. Unfortunately, time and time again defendants go to prison after violating one or more terms of their probation.

Often these "violations" are technical, i.e. not criminal acts. Life happens, and sometimes things get rough; however, that is not a sufficient excuse for violating a term of your probation or failing to attend a class or complete community service. This is just one of the reasons why I fight so hard to get the most reasonable terms of probation for my clients, and encourage them to complete the terms they can before we resolve their case.

Often, criminal defendants are so happy to have their case behind them they forget the importance of staying on top of their probation, which is why my firm goes over the terms of probation with every client before the day we resolve the clients case; the day of/before the plea; and after sentencing. Additionally, I encourage clients to meet with their probation officer early and often to ensure both are on the same page.

ATTRIBUTES OF A GREAT CRIMINAL DEFENSE LAW FIRM

Cannon Law Firm is not a general practice law firm. We defend Citizens and Soldiers facing criminal charges and contested family law matters. You want to hire a law firm that specializes in only a few areas of practice, with substantial experience in criminal defense. You should hire a law firm with attorneys that have existing, positive, professional relationships with the individuals they come in contact with on your behalf in your case.

The law firm you hire should not only have years of experience, but years of handling complex and challenging criminal defense cases across the state and at every level of the criminal justice system. Many attorneys have "decades of experience", but how many years have they practiced criminal defense? How many criminal defense cases do they handle every year? How many criminal defense cases have they handled in their career? How many criminal jury trials have they conducted? Were they first or second chair attorney in those cases? Your case and your future are in better hands with a Law Firm and an attorney that has handled the cases of over 1,000 criminal defendants across the spectrum of criminal justice. Cannon Law Firm is that law firm.

There are pros and cons to the accessibility of online marketing in today's legal market. An attorney can get substantial exposure without the experience necessary to competently defend individuals facing serious charges; however, if you look hard enough you will find the truth about their experience and expertise. You want a law firm and attorney visible online with a professional website, but your research should not stop there. Seek out and view their reviews, YouTube channel, their written and video blogs, their social media posts, and the testimonials of their former clients.

You will be starting with a disadvantage if you hire a criminal defense law firm without a great reputation. The business organization of the law firm you retain is crucial to your success. When cases and clients stack up or trial is upon them, a law firm with procedures will efficiently stay on top of all their clients' cases, a disorganized law firm will not.

There is no faster way to learn about the character and caliber of your potential attorney than former client reviews and testimonials. You will be better served by hiring an attorney with a large number of good-to-great reviews than an attorney with only three or four perfect scores. Attorney recognition matters to lawyers and it should matter to you as a potential client. Has the attorney you are considering received peer-reviewed awards? Is there a vetting process for the awards he/she has received? Attorney awards function similar to other professions, so pay attention. The absence of any awards may be a reason to consider continuing your search for your attorney.

Some law firms undercut competing firms, regardless of the true value or cost to defend a specific type of case. You want to hire a law firm that is happy to represent you, but does not 'need' your business. Hiring a criminal defense attorney can be a confusing and sometimes scary experience. When you or a loved one's future and freedom hang in the balance it is crucial you retain the right counsel. The best way to address this concern is by doing your homework: seek opinions, read reviews, visit websites, interview law firms, and trust your gut. Meet a few firms and hire the best criminal defense law firm you can afford.

This is one of the most important decisions you will make, do not take it lightly. Hiring the attorney with the lowest price is never good for your case or future. You get what you pay for in criminal defense law firms, as with many things in life. Observe the law firm you consider hiring, how they conduct business will be indicative of how they will handle your case, your future, and your life.

CANNON LAW FIRM: SET APART

Few criminal defense attorneys have handled the number and caliber of criminal cases that I have in my career to this point. However, that is not the only reason to consider hiring my Firm. My clients benefit every day from the way in which I conduct business and my dedication to every client throughout the particular process they are facing.

I constantly strive to reach the best possible outcome for every client, through Fierce Advocacy and dedication to each individual client's case. Every client I represent, from a simple possession of drugs charge to Murder in the First Degree, deserves and receives dedicated detail oriented service from my Firm.

I consider representing a client be an honor and responsibility, which my firm takes very seriously. My Firm treats every client and potential client as a person with a life beyond their case, with hopes and dreams beyond their current circumstance. Our analysis of your case does not begin with or end with your charges, it is about you: your past, your present, and your future. We are dedicated to identifying client's greatest fears and finding a way to protect clients from that fear becoming your reality. We cannot obtain every goal for every client, but we strive to ensure every client understands every step of the process and feels their desires are respected, which is our central focus in representing that client. My Firm strives to be attorney and counselor at law. You are more than a number and a criminal case at my Firm.

CONCLUSION

Always bear in mind that your own resolution to succeed is more important than any other one thing – Abraham Lincoln

I hope this book has answered some of the questions you and your family have in facing a criminal investigation or charges in Oklahoma State, Federal, and Military Courts. At the least, this book should have provided you with information about what you are facing, and making a well-informed decision in hiring an experienced Oklahoma criminal defense law.

I wish you and yours the best in this process and beyond. Please let us know, if we can be of assistance. What was true in Abraham Lincoln's time one-hundred and fifty years ago is true today: *Your dedication to getting past this difficult time in life means more than any adversity you are facing.* I wish you the best through the process you are facing. Please feel free to contact my Firm for a free and confidential consultation.

INDEX

A	N
Affidavit and Notice of Revocation	Nolo Contendre
Alleged	
APC	
Arraignment	
Arrest Process	
Assault & Battery Crimes	
B	**O**
Bail Slip	Offense Characteristics
BAC	Offense Levels
Better Business Bureau	
Bureau of Alcohol, Tobacco, Firearms and Explosives	Order of Revocation
	O.R. Bond
Bondsman	
Book-In	
Burden Of Proof	
C	**P**
Case Evaluation	Plea
Case Law	Plea Agreement

Cash Bond Certification Hearing Characterization Of Service (Military) Circumstantial Evidence Citation Clients Closing Argument Community Confinement Community Intervention Center Complaint Conditional Bond Constitutional Rights Regarding Arrest Convening Authorities Court-Martial Criminal Defense Attorney Criminal Charges Criminal History Category Cross-examine	Police Post-Trial Motions Preemptory Challenges Preliminary Hearing Pretrial Conference Presentence Report Privilege Prosecutors Probable Cause Property Crimes Public Defenders
D Defense Deferred Sentence Department of Public	Q

Safety Department of Veterans Affairs Direct Evidence Dismissal (Of Charges) Discovery Process Diversion Programs Drug Enforcement Administration Drug Offenses Due Process Drug Schedules DUI/DWI	
E Evidence Exculpatory Evidence Extenuating Circumstances	R Reasonable Doubt Restitution
F Federal Investigations Federal Bureau of Investigation Federal District Judge Federal Sentencing Guidelines Felony	S Search Warrant Sealed Proceeding Securities and Exchange Commission Sentencing Sexual Assault Schedule Shock Incarceration

	Skills Education Program
	Statute Title
	Statutory Reference
	Storytelling
	Suppression
	Suspended Sentence
G Grand Jury Guilty Plea	**T** Testimony Testimonials The Information Trial
H Home Detention Homeland Security Investigations	**U** Uniform Code of Military Justice United States Attorneys United States Code United States Marshals United States Secret Service Unjustified Gain
I Impeach Implied Consent Implied Consent Revocation Incarceration In Custody	**V** Venire Verdict Veteran Diversion Programs Victim Voir Dire

Indictment Initial Hearing Internal Revenue Service Intermittent Confinement Interrogation Investigation	
J Judge Advocate Jurisdiction Jury Deliberation Jury Instructions Jury Selection Jury Trial Justice System Juvenile Criminal Defense Juvenile Delinquent	W Waive Walk-Through Warrant White Collar Crime Witnesses
K Kidnapping	X
L Larceny Letter of Support Litigation	Y Youthful Offender Youthful Offender Act

M	Z
Magistrate Judge Mental Health Courts Military Justice System Misdemeanor Miranda Rights Mitigating Circumstances Modified Driver's License Motion Practice Murder	

TESTIMONIALS (CONT.)

"Mr. Cannon has represented me on 2 criminal cases and one civil case over the past 4 years. He has always served me honestly, speedily and with good moral direction. John has integrity and humility. He has never belittled me or treated me in an unfair manner. I appreciate all that he has done for me and I most certainly recommend him to family, strangers and friends. I will definitely use Mr. Cannon in the future for any and all of my family's legal matters."

Candice

****

"John is a highly respected attorney. Professional and compassionate. He has a wealth of knowledge, being a military officer and having served as an Assistant District Attorney, a Public Defender, and an Assistant Attorney General. He helped a friend's son who was headed down the wrong path, but through John's legal defense the young man is now a successful business owner."

Attorney Colleague

****

"John Cannon is an amazing attorney. During one of the most difficult times of my life he showed compassion, was honest, and patiently answered my questions."

Sharon

****

"John is a very professional attorney, who is not only concerned about the welfare of his client but very attentive and considerate of the family, or other bodies that are in the face of the adversity. While working on my family member's case, John took time out to take a class that would educate him on how to approach the many different types of cases tried in the court room. John proved his sincerity to the calling of his job, being an attorney. I would definitely recommend him to anyone."

Laquita

****

"Mr. Cannon went above and beyond for my wife. She was facing some pretty hard fines and prison time with the US Marshals. Mr. Cannon fought a hard fight and got her a GREAT offer. Words cannot express how much I appreciate him and what he did for my wife. I would give 10 stars and I will be promoting him. He's that awesome. He keeps you informed, he will text or call you back, and he goes above what he is asked to do and I can reassure you. HE WILL FIGHT FOR YOU OR YOUR FAMILY MEMBER. I will continue retaining him for other things my wife is battling. High five and a great big hug to Mr. Cannon. Thank you!!! John took the reigns and provided us instant peace of mind. He was timely, respectful, transparent, very professional, honest and courteous. The service he provided was above and beyond our expectations. Can't believe professionals like him are around. Highly highly without reservations recommend him and his team."

Tara

****

"My experience with Cannon Law Firm was absolutely amazing. I hired John Cannon two days before my rebuttal statement was due back to the Staff Judge Advocate. Within that time frame he was able to talk to my Battery and Battalion Commanders, review my evidence, and help me write a rebuttal statement that helped prove my case to them, the Brigade Commander and the Post Commanding General. Cannon worked thru the night to help me get the best results for me and my family. Due to his hard work and attention to detail I am still able to continue to serve my country and progress in my military career with no adverse actions on my record. I cannot thank him enough on a job well done. Cannon showed me that he was invested in my case and I highly recommend you hire him when you need someone to represent you in a legal matter."

Zavien

****

"Counsel John Cannon was flawless in every way in my case. Defendant & family had so much first time fears about the court process, etc. due to this client's first time ever DUI crime, at the age of 60 years old. Thankfully attorney John Cannon could not have more perfectly represented this client. 100% referral suggested!! Highly so."

Hubert

About the Author

HUSBAND, FATHER, SOLDIER, AND COUNSELOR

John is dedicated to helping you and your family through the difficult situation you are facing. He will be your Fierce Advocate, while always keeping you informed. It is important to have competent and caring counsel by your side from the first moment you believe charges may be filed until your case is complete.

Some ask, "why do you practice criminal defense?" John always gives the same answer; *he is passionate about taking care of and fighting alongside people facing the most difficult time in their life and defending those accused of serious crimes*. The protections of the Constitution mean nothing, if we do not hold the government to those standards in even the most abominable cases.

From the beginning of law school, John has been dedicated to trial advocacy and fighting for his clients. In law school, he participated in an international law and trial advocacy program in Germany, and has not stopped trying challenging cases ever since. John gained further criminal law experience as an Assistant District Attorney prosecuting complex cases from investigation through trial. Subsequently, he became an Assistant Public Defender in Oklahoma County, handling a felony docket and representing clients through every aspect of the criminal justice system, including jury trial and appeals before the Oklahoma Court of Criminal Appeals.

Next, John expanded his experience by becoming an Assistant Attorney General, representing the State of Oklahoma in state and federal court, including arguing before the Tenth Circuit Court of Appeals. He left the Office of the Attorney General to open his own criminal defense practice, Cannon Law Firm, PLLC.

John's practice extends to his military service. He has achieved the Army rank of Major and continues to serve Soldiers as a Judge Advocate in the Oklahoma National Guard. He has defended Soldiers in all aspects of the military justice system in a reserve and active duty status. He has tried Court-Martials at Fort Bragg, Fort Sill, Vance Air Force Base, and represented Soldiers during active duty service in Washington, D.C. He continues to serve as Deputy Staff Judge Advocate for the National Guard. He has advised and represented countless Soldiers in all types of criminal and administrative actions.

John has received numerous peer nominated and reviewed awards, including: The National Trial Lawyers 40 under 40 Award in Criminal Defense. He prides himself in being a Fierce Advocate for every client he serves.

John's experience and reputation will be an asset for you during this difficult time. The Cannon Law Firm strives to give every client all the information available at every step of their case and ensure each and every client understands his or her options before any decision. Cannon Law Firm is ready to help you!

Finally, we wish you and yours the very best in this difficult time and we are ready and willing to meet with you for a free completely confidential consultation to discuss your case and the next step in defending your case and freedom.

www.ingramcontent.com/pod-product-compliance
Lightning Source LLC
Chambersburg PA
CBHW030006190526
45157CB00014B/670